WHAT PEOPLE ARE SAYIN

DO WE NEED GOD TO BE GOOD?

The 'God Debate' is alive and kicking as never before, and Christopher Hallpike's book is a significant contribution to our understanding of New Atheism, morality, religion and reason. Lively and highly stimulating, it offers an engaging and thought-provoking account that will generate much debate and discussion, and is an excellent book for anyone seeking to understand some of the key philosophical, moral and religious issues of our time.

Professor Martyn Percy, Dean of Christ Church, Oxford

A beautifully written, deceptively effortless survey of a vast literature on many of the ultimate questions that face humanity. It is a most impressive achievement, and all within such a mercifully manageable compass.

Dr Henry Hardy, Fellow of Wolfson College Oxford. Editor of the writings of Isaiah Berlin

Do We Need God to Be Good?

An anthropologist considers the evidence

Do We Need God to Be Good?

An anthropologist considers the evidence

C. R. Hallpike

Winchester, UK
Washington, USA

First published by Circle Books, 2016
Circle Books is an imprint of John Hunt Publishing Ltd., Laurel House, Station Approach,
Alresford, Hants, SO24 9JH, UK
office1@jhpbooks.net
www.johnhuntpublishing.com
www.circle-books.com

For distributor details and how to order please visit the 'Ordering' section on our website.

Text copyright: C. R. Hallpike 2015

ISBN: 978 1 78535 217 1
Library of Congress Control Number: 2015946045

A CIP catalogue record for this book is available from the British Library.

Design: Lee Nash

Printed and bound by CPI Group (UK) Ltd, Croydon, CR0 4YY, UK

We operate a distinctive and ethical publishing philosophy in all
areas of our business, from our global network of authors to
production and worldwide distribution.

CONTENTS

Acknowledgements

I am most grateful to my daughter Julia, the Revd Canon Andrew Bowden, Prof Jonathan Good, Dr Henry Hardy, and Alison Hull for their comments and support.

C.R.H.
Shipton Moyne
Gloucestershire
June 2015

Introduction

If we all stopped believing in God, what effect would this have on our ideas of right and wrong, and how we should live? According to atheists the result would be a thoroughly good thing, because in their view reason and evidence are all we need to guide our moral choices, and atheists certainly don't need God to be good. But religion, according to them, is ancient superstition that rejects reason, has encouraged wars, hatred, and persecution throughout history, and clouds our judgement and warps our lives with a morbid sense of guilt. As the slogan on the London buses put it: "There's probably no God. Now stop worrying and enjoy your life."[1] Instead of being oppressed by religious taboos and the arbitrary commandments of a supposed God, modern secular society believes it has discovered by reason and evidence how to build a tolerant, liberal way of life. There is the comfortable assumption that if only God could be removed from the scene then our society, complete of course with human rights, could continue happily on its way, no longer disturbed by the irrational taboos and hatreds fostered by religion now and throughout history.

But modern atheism is actually driven by evolutionary biology, which takes us into the very different world of the Darwinian struggle for survival, in which we are no different from animals, and of materialist fundamentalism. Because atheists assume that matter is the only thing that exists this not only abolishes God and the supernatural but also abolishes us, at least in the traditional sense of possessing consciousness, identity, and free will, so that we cease to be moral beings at all. Humanists carefully avoid mentioning all this, but if one actually takes the full implications of atheism seriously the kinds of value system and society that can be built on it are going to be very much darker than most people would care to face, with no place

1

for liberal ideals, human rights, or toleration. This book does not attempt the impossible task of *proving* the existence of God, but at least it can demonstrate the logical consequences of unbelief more clearly and atheists need to recognise how unpleasant these are likely to be. My argument will be about principles and 'world-views', however, not about the character and behaviour of individuals. To claim that religious belief automatically makes people good, while atheism makes them bad is ridiculous and is no part of my argument.

This begins in Chapter 1 with human nature for two reasons. First, we need to see how it lays some of the foundations for moral – and immoral – behaviour. We have to understand the basics of human co-operation and conflict, and the minimum requirements for a viable social life, and we can do this without any reference to religion. Darwin was correct in claiming not only that we evolved from an earlier form of primate, but that there are important emotional continuities from animals to humans which provide *some* of the essential ingredients for human morality. Secondly, evolutionary biologists make sweeping claims that since Darwin they are now the experts we should trust to explain human nature and ethics, and that their theories have made all others obsolete.

But evolutionary biologists are not the only scientists who can claim to have special insights into the human condition, and for more than a hundred years social anthropologists have been collecting a mass of evidence about the human race in all its variety around the world. As an anthropologist myself I have spent my life living with remote tribes in the mountains of Ethiopia and Papua New Guinea and learning their languages, writing books about them, and generally researching the way of life of non-Western peoples, particularly those of tribal societies. While evolutionary biologists are very fond of referring to these societies when discussing prehistoric humans, this usually takes the form of armchair speculation based on very little anthropological knowledge. But how do the claims of evolutionary biology really stand up in the face of anthropological scrutiny? Although some of their contributions to the study of human nature are reasonable and illuminating, others go well beyond Darwin and are the product of a materialist world-view with a deeply anti-human agenda, rather than of objective and evidence-based science.[2]

Anthropologists have also learned a good deal about the varieties of religion and human moral systems, which we come to in the second chapter. Here it needs to be remembered that the simpler, non-literate societies traditionally studied by anthropologists are far more typical of the human race than modern industrialised societies, which have only been around for a few generations. Atheist stereotypes of religion as nothing more than a survival of ancient beliefs in supernatural beings, and of religious morality as unthinking obedience to the arbitrary commandments of these inscrutable deities, are uninformed, and ignore the ways in which religion has changed and developed from its earlier forms to those we find in the world religions. The second chapter is therefore an anthropological account of what religion is about and how it has evolved in some fundamental respects, and shows that a system of ethics based on advanced forms of religion must be systematically different in some respects from a purely secular one.

In fact, religion does make distinctive and essential contributions to morality after all, though not necessarily in ways that it is popularly supposed to do. Here, it is essential to understand in the first place that our *basic* moral ideas such as helping others and fairness don't come from God at all, but from our experience of living in society and from our human nature. To this extent we can indeed be good without God. The world religions, however, go further than our social experience: they assume that the universe makes sense and that we have a special place in it, and make their distinctive contribution to the *higher* aspects of ethics, in such ideas as the superiority of spiritual over material values, humility and selflessness, the brotherhood of man, and the moral dignity of the individual, and religious morality often goes against human nature and the pressures of society.

In the third chapter we come to Humanism, the most popular form of atheist morality, and we find that its picture of religion is generally a caricature that is not based on any real attempt to consider the evidence. In particular, religion is not necessarily hostile to science, but historically has actually been one of its essential foundations. In examining the claims of Humanism to provide an alternative, secular, system of ethics we discover that it is really just a *resumé* of fashionable Western liberalism, and glorifies pride and worldly success. Although they are enormously enthusiastic about human rights, and regard them as the secular replacement of the Gospels and far superior to the teachings of Christ, Humanists do not realise that they were originally the product of Christian civilisation. In the Darwinian world of nature, however, which they claim is the only one, there can be no such things as rights, either for humans or for animals, but only the struggle for survival in which we have no more significance than ants or wasps.

Finally, in Chapter 4, we look at some genuinely atheist systems of ethics that have been worked out in modern times. Earlier, I pointed out that religion helps maintain the proper balance between the mutual claims of the individual and society by the mediation of the Divine, which stands outside and above all social orders. Without God, who legitimises the moral demands of the social order, on the one hand, but who also sanctifies the dignity of the individual, on the other, there will be inevitable social pressures either to develop unrestricted individualism, or unrestricted totalitarianism, the worship either of the Self or the State, or merely of Power itself. Here we see how this works out in practice in a variety of atheist moral systems.

Chapter 1

Human Nature

The question 'What is man?' is probably the most profound that can be asked by man. It has always been central to any system of philosophy or theology... The point I want to make now is that all attempts to answer that question before 1859 [Darwin's *Origin of Species*] are worthless and we will be better off if we ignore them completely. (Simpson 1966:472)

1. Evolutionary psychologists in the Garden of Eden

Religious fundamentalists believe that every word of the Bible is literally true. Since it says that God created Adam and Eve, our first parents, in the Garden of Eden the claims by Charles Darwin and biologists since his day that we evolved over millions of years from ancient ape-like creatures therefore can't be true. But these 'Creationists' don't seem to have noticed that while the Book of Genesis does say that God created Adam and Eve, it also (1.6-10) requires us to believe that the earth is flat, surrounded by the waters below the solid sky, or firmament, (the standard theory in the ancient world). Even Creationists might feel rather awkward about defending this view in public, but if they believe in the literal truth of the Bible it is hard to see how they could deny it. The Church actually abandoned the primitive idea of a flat earth quite early in its history, and in AD 415, for example, St Augustine wrote a treatise *On the Literal Interpretation of Genesis*, in which he argued that the Bible was about faith and morals and not a science text-book, and that whether one thought the earth was round or flat was entirely irrelevant to salvation. His argument that the Bible and science are quite distinct sources of authority was later quoted by Galileo against the Inquisition, and no anthropologist could take the mythical account of human

5

origins in Genesis as serious science. (Myths can convey important truths, but they are not intended as literal fact.)

DNA evidence, in particular, gives compelling support to the basic Darwinian claim that humans evolved from a pre-human life-form over millions of years in East Africa. Biologists, on the other hand, are in the habit of inflating the significance of this and claiming that everything about how we think and behave can be explained as adaptations to prehistoric life in East Africa.

The first problem is that the *detailed* evidence about the seven million years or so during which our ancestors evolved from the Common Ancestor of the African great apes and ourselves into *Homo sapiens* is remarkably small. (The skeletal evidence itself, though of great importance, would fit in the boot of a car.) Even such basic adaptive problems as why we came to walk upright, why we began to use tools, why we lost our hairy coats, why our brains expanded disproportionately to our body size, why alone among all species we came to use fire to cook our food, and how we acquired language are still hotly debated.

'Evolutionary psychologists', who claim that our human abilities and traits are very specific adaptations to the problems of pre-historic life on the savannah in East Africa, have not faced up to the fact that we know virtually nothing about what this life involved, about the social relations and organisation of our ancestors in those remote epochs, and still less about their mental capacities. If we are going to use the theory of natural selection to explain the characteristics of any species, it is obviously essential to have a detailed knowledge of their behaviour in relation to their environment. In the case of a social species it is particularly important to observe the relations between individuals, and modern studies of chimpanzees and gorillas are obvious examples of how this should be done. But while it is reasonable to assume that our ancestors in this remote period lived in very small groups of gatherers and scavenger/hunters, and to deduce from this that we must have been an innately sociable species for a very long time, and that some of the well-established gender differences seem to be adaptations to this way of life, it is difficult to be sure about much else. Normal science proceeds from the known to the unknown, but evolutionary psychology tries to do it the other way round.

Language is central to human culture, but we do not even know when our ancestors were first able to utter sentences like 'Shall we go hunting tomorrow?', and it is quite possible that they only achieved this level of linguistic ability well within the last 100,000 years or so. But without language there would have been no way of referring to the future or the past, no means of conveying information, no group planning, no way of communicating group norms and ideas of sharing and cheating, and no discussion of technology and other problems of survival. We cannot even imagine what a pre-linguistic human society might have been like. It cannot be sufficiently emphasized, therefore, that our profound ignorance about early humans is quite incompatible with any informed discussion of possible adaptations.

Even in the case of the earliest *Homo sapiens sapiens* from around 200,000 years ago we do not know what sort of things they might have said to each other, (or if they could have said much at all), what made them laugh, or even if they laughed, what they quarrelled about or how they organised sharing within the group. Nor do we have any idea when they first had personal names, or when they could form the ideas of 'grandfather', or 'mother's brother', or when they developed the idea of some sort of official union between adult men and women, or if they exchanged women between bands, or how hunting cooperation was organized, or what sort of leadership existed. Nor do we know when humans first had ideas of magic and symbolism, gods, ghosts, and spirits, or when or why they first performed religious rituals and disposed of the dead in a more than merely physical manner.

Ignoring these drastic limitations on our knowledge has

meant that many so-called 'adaptive explanations' are merely pseudo-scientific 'Just So Stories', often made up without any anthropological knowledge, that have increasingly brought evolutionary psychology into disrepute. For example, it has been claimed (in the *Proceedings of the Royal Society*[1] no less) that more than a million years ago, early humans lost their body hair because it was full of nasty parasites, and potential mates therefore preferred partners with the least amount of hair so that it was eliminated by sexual selection. Instead of body hair, humans took to wearing clothes: 'clothes, unlike fur, can be changed and cleaned'.[2] We know nothing whatsoever about the sexual preferences of our ancestors a million years ago, but at least we know they could not possibly have had clothes, because these have only been around for a few thousand years since the introduction of farming and weaving.[3] Another example of an adaptive theory, recently published in *New Scientist*[4], is obviously based on the author's experience of living in London rather than on any anthropological knowledge about hunter-gatherers. 'The first, and most ancient function of manners is to solve the problem of how to be social without getting sick [from other people's germs].' No it isn't. If there was a 'first and most ancient function of manners' it would have been to reduce social friction among small groups of people who have to live and get along with one another, and a hunter-gatherer band was, in any case, the environment where one had the least chance in human history of catching a disease from someone else.[5] Some years previously, *New Scientist* also published an evolutionary expla-nation of nightmares: 'In the ancestral environment human life was short and full of threats', so that 'A dream-production mechanism that tends to select threatening events, and to simulate them over and over again in various combinations, would have been valuable for the development of threat-avoiding skills'. Since most people wake up screaming when the threat comes, however, nightmares seem a most unpromising educational tool. And as I write, yet another evolutionary knee-slapper has appeared, in *Biological Reviews*[6], this time maintaining that men's faces and jaws are more robust than women's because for millions of years men have engaged in fist fights. The problem here is that we know from anthropological studies that hunter-gatherers are not recorded as engaging in fist fights but in physical conflicts typically use weapons like clubs, spears, or rocks because they are so much more effective than trying to use one's bare hands. Boxing as such is a skill that has to be deliberately taught and is only found in a small minority of societies which makes it extremely unlikely that it was an important form of human combat for millions of years.

The second problem is that if our ancestors were so closely adapted to the environment of prehistoric East Africa, this should be able to tell us a great deal about their subsequent behaviour, especially during the last 10,000 years of maximal social and cultural change. For example, we would expect humans, in their expansion all over the globe, to have chosen environments with a discernible resemblance to the savannah of East Africa[7], and to have avoided those that differed markedly from it, like rain-forests, deserts, the arctic, islands in the Pacific Ocean, and high mountain ranges. We would also expect them, after millions of years of simple, egalitarian hunter-gatherer existence in small groups, to have been strongly resistant to the formation of large-scale, highly stratified societies, and again to have had great difficulty in mastering mathematics, science, and modern electronic technology, just to mention a few glaring examples of major cultural change. Yet we know very well that in these and innumerable other respects, human habitats, social organisation, culture, technology and modes of thought have diverged in wildly different ways from the simple model of Man in his prehistoric environment, so that evolutionary psychology has no predictive value at all in these essential respects. This alone makes it very unlikely that human abilities and dispositions were ever closely adapted to particular ancestral conditions. 'Among the multitude of animals which scamper, fly, burrow and swim around us, man is the only one who is not locked into his environment. His imagination, his reason, his emotional subtlety and toughness, make it possible for him not to accept the environment but to change it.'[8]

Thirdly, Man's extraordinary intellectual abilities, in particular, raise the problem that in Darwinian theory biological adaptations can only be to *existing* circumstances, never to those that might be encountered in the future. We did not acquire our mathematical abilities, for example, so that thousands of years later we could be good with computers. This fundamental point about human abilities was first made by A.R.Wallace, Darwin's co-formulator of the theory of natural selection, who had extensive first-hand acquaintance with hunter-gatherers of the Amazon and south-east Asia. He noted that on the one hand their mode of life made only very limited intellectual demands on them, and did not require abstract concepts of number and geometry, space, time, music, and advanced ethical principles, yet as individuals they were potentially capable of mastering the highly demanding cognitive skills of modern industrial civili-sation if they were given the chance to acquire them. Since, as noted, natural selection can only produce traits that are adapted to existing, and not future, conditions, it 'could only have endowed savage man with a brain a little superior to that of an ape, where he actually possesses one little inferior to that of a philosopher'.[9]

This is particularly obvious in the case of mathematics, where even today many simple cultures, especially hunter-gatherers but including some shifting cultivators may only have words for single, pair, and many. The Tauade of Papua New Guinea with whom I lived were like this, and indeed, the hunter-gatherer Piraha of South America are described[10] as having no number words at all, not even the grammatical distinction between singular and plural. We can get a good idea why this should be so from the example of a Cree hunter from eastern Canada: he was asked in a court case involving land how many rivers there were in his hunting territory, and did not know:

> The hunter knew every river in his territory individually and therefore had no need to know how many there were. Indeed, he would know each stretch of each river as an individual thing and therefore had no need to know in numerical terms how long the rivers were. The point of the story is that we count things when we are ignorant of their individual identity – this can arise when we don't have enough experience of the objects, when there are too many of them to know individually, or when they are all the same, none of which conditions obtain very often for a hunter. If he has several knives they will be known individually by their different sizes, shapes, and specialized uses. If he has several pairs of moccasins they will be worn to different degrees, having been made at different times, and may be of different materials and design.[11]

What needs to be emphasised here, therefore, is that our hunter-gatherer ancestors could easily have survived without the need for verbal numerals or for any counting at all, and that consequently there could have been no selective pressure for arithmetical skills to evolve in the specific conditions of the Pleistocene of East Africa. As we all know, mathematics has only flowered in the last few centuries, and among a tiny minority of people, far too brief a time-span for natural selection to have had the least effect. The mathematician Keith Devlin very reasonably concludes: 'Whatever features of our brain enable (some of) us to do mathematics must have been present long before we had any mathematics. *Those crucial features, therefore, must have evolved to fulfil some other purpose'* (my emphasis).[12] Because we have no idea what that 'other purpose' might have been we are obviously not going to discover the origin of the mathematical features of the human brain from anything we suppose our ancestors might have been doing in pre-history.

Mathematics is only one particularly glaring example of a whole range of advanced human thought in logic, philosophy, and science, of a type known as 'formal operations', which has only emerged in literate civilisations, and is never found among hunter-gatherers. This general type of thought must therefore be the result, like mathematics, of the brain using its faculties in novel ways, which therefore cannot be traced back to African prehistory.

So while Man has clearly evolved from non-human primates, speculation by evolutionary psychologists about how modern human nature and abilities might be adaptations to what our ancestors' life on the African savannah might, or might not, have been like, has contributed remarkably little to science. Here we have learnt vastly more by studying living people around us today, as we shall see in the next section.

2. Co-operation and altruism

In the twentieth century, as part of their opposition to racial theories, anthropologists in particular adopted the highly implausible view that there is no such thing as human nature and that all aspects of human behaviour, even the differences between the sexes, are simply the results of the particular culture in which we have grown up. According to Clifford Geertz, 'There is no such thing as a human nature independent of culture'[13], and the only thing that can be said about human nature is that 'it is unbelievably malleable', to quote Margaret Mead.

This contradicted a long intellectual tradition in Western thought that there is indeed a human nature and that it is fundamentally selfish. The Social Contract theory of Locke and Hobbes, for example, was based on this view of human nature, and assumed that government and the state were established by essentially selfish individuals only because the cost of conflict had become unbearable. (Aristotle, on the contrary, had supposed that we were inherently social.) In Freud's view, the Id was what we were naturally, the oldest and most primitive part of the personality, basically anti-social and driven to satisfy the primal instincts of sex and aggression. Again, a long individualist tradition in economics has assumed that we are basically rational individuals who act entirely out of our own self-interest, with the aim of maximising our own gains in every situation, and the extremely influential Rawlsian model of justice also takes it for granted that we should think of society essentially in terms of competing individuals. This individualist model of human nature has been reinforced since the 1960s by evolutionary biologists claiming that we must be fundamentally selfish, since any altruistic impulses of individuals to sacrifice their own welfare for that of others would have been weeded out by natural selection. (This was in marked contrast to the earlier view of biologists that successful *groups*, as well as individuals, would be selected for.) Richard Dawkins has put the modern view very clearly:

The argument of this book is that we, and all other animals, are machines created by our genes. Like successful Chicago gangsters, our genes have survived, in some cases for millions of years, in a highly competitive world. This entitles us to expect certain qualities in our genes. I shall argue that a predominant quality to be expected in a successful gene is ruthless selfishness. This gene selfishness will usually give rise to selfishness in individual behaviour... Be warned that if you wish, as I do, to build a society in which individuals co-operate generously and unselfishly towards a common good, you can expect little help from biological nature. Let us try to teach generosity and altruism, because we are born selfish. Let us understand what our own selfish genes are up to, because we may then at least have the chance to upset their designs, something which no other species has ever aspired to.[14]

How we can be 'born selfish' but at the same time hope to upset our genes' designs and become altruists is not discussed. But he goes on to explain, (popularising the work of the biologist Bill Hamilton, and his theory of kin selection, or inclusive fitness), that we are actually programmed by natural selection to maximize the reproductive success of our *genes*, and so we can only be altruistic to other people if they are our kin like siblings, nephews, or close cousins. This 'nepotism' makes evolutionary sense because they, too, share some of our genes and in assisting them we are helping to propagate those genes we have in common. The leading biologist Richard Alexander therefore concluded that human societies are nothing more than collections of individuals seeking their own self-interest, and our belief that normal people will sometimes make sacrifices to help non-relatives and strangers is not supported by a shred of evidence.[15] He claimed that inclusive fitness theory resolves 'the ancient philosophical paradox whether humans are really selfish individualists or group altruists, and provided, I believe, the first simple, general theory of human nature with a high likelihood of widespread acceptance', and asserted that the theory could never be disproved or even need revision.

This confidence turned out to be rather premature, however, since more recent research has shown that individual altruism can easily evolve in situations where *several groups are in competition*. While selfishness will beat altruism within a group, if altruists and non-altruists are concentrated in different groups, the groups with more altruists will be at a competitive advantage over the groups with fewer altruists, and will therefore grow larger than them.[16] Darwin's belief in group, as well as individual, selection has therefore been vindicated. The theory that an inherently social species such as Man could nevertheless be basically selfish was always thoroughly implausible anyway, and Alexander could provide no convincing explanation of how a species of selfish individualists has nevertheless managed to live in societies of many millions.

At this point I should also stress that the biologists' assumption of a clear conflict between selfishness and altruism does not have nearly as much relevance to human society as it does to animal groups. Not only can much human co-operation be explained by enlightened self-interest – co-operation in a task may clearly be to everyone's benefit, one's reputation may suffer if one does not help, and so on – but giving significant help to others may involve little or no cost to the donor. This is especially true of information, one of the unique features of human society, as in warning someone about a poisonous plant.

But it is also quite clear that we have evolved a natural disposition to help one another out of sympathy[17], and we should note the importance of sympathy and kindness as one of the essential foundations of ethical behaviour. A wide range of animals, too, are clearly capable of this as we know from the friendship between ourselves and our pets, for example, and sympathy probably first emerged as an aspect of parental care.[18]

In this sense of mutual kindness and co-operation we need not hesitate, therefore, to agree with biologists that we have inherited some essential features of moral behaviour from our mammalian ancestors. But feelings alone do not constitute morality in the human sense, and the co-operation involved in human society and morality involves distinctively human *cognitive* processes as well as sentiments, as we shall now see.

Modern experimental research has repeatedly confirmed what we have always known: that while human beings can indeed be selfish, aggressive, and competitive they are also innately co-operative and pro-social, regardless of kinship and nepotism, (and are quite distinct from apes in this respect). It is of course true that 'All viable organisms must have a selfish streak; they must be concerned about their own survival and well-being or they will not be leaving many offspring. But human co-operation and helpfulness are, as it were, laid on top of this self-interested foundation' (Tomasello 2009:4-5). Professor Tomasello's comparative research at the Max Planck Institute of Evolutionary Anthropology in Leipzig, conducted on infants of 12 to 24 months, and on chimpanzees, has confirmed that, unlike apes, 'To an unprecedented degree, *Homo sapiens* are adapted for acting and thinking co-operatively in cultural groups...' (xv). Inclusive fitness theorists concentrate almost entirely on gift-giving as the test of altruism, but Tomasello points out that this is far too narrow not only because it should include assistance and information, but because altruism is only one part of a much more comprehensive pattern of *cognitively-based* collaboration and mutual assistance, and an atmosphere of tolerance and trust that is innate and uniquely human.

Human infants start co-operating at about a year, and when 14-18 month-old infants were put in situations where adult strangers needed help with a variety of problems, like picking up something they had dropped, or opening a cupboard door, the infants spontaneously helped them. 'To help others flexibly in these ways, infants need, first, to be able to perceive others' goals in a variety of situations, and second to have the altruistic motive to help them' (7). This behaviour emerges very early without training. Parental rewards do not increase infant helpfulness but actually inhibit it, and it occurs cross-culturally. Very young children may also offer to share, and the tendency to share increases with age, being accompanied by a rapid growth in the capacity for empathy.

Again, 'teaching is a form of altruism, founded on a motive to help, in which individuals donate information to others for their use' (xiv), and humans actively teach each other things without regard to kinship. Even before speech develops, infants will try to provide information to adult strangers who need it by pointing, but apes do not understand this type of informative pointing at all. They do sometimes point at humans, but only to indicate that they want something for themselves; on the other hand, 'Confronted with pointing, [human] infants appear to ask themselves "why does *she* think that my attending to that cup will be helpful or relevant to *me*?"' (18).

Infants also have an innate grasp of rules, in the sense of readily understanding that things *should* be done in a certain way, and try to enforce this. Children therefore legislate norms by themselves, regardless of parental instruction, even when not immediately involved in an activity, so that, observing a solitary game, they will condemn a puppet who is introduced and then disobeys the rules. The notion of the ideal way of how a game ought to be played follows directly from watching an adult, and children don't need to see the adult corrected. So rules are not just instrumental guides to the children's own effective action, but 'are supra-individual entities that carry social force independently of such instrumental considerations' (38). Children's earliest norms (at around 3 years) are therefore true social norms, and they result from something more than either the fear of authority or the promise of reciprocity. These cannot, in particular, account for the child's active enforcement of social norms, since they are not taught to do this (39).

For this degree of co-ordination and communication to be possible, the participants must therefore have (1) a joint goal in the sense that they, in mutual knowledge, do X together, and (2) the participants must co-ordinate their roles which are interdependent, and this requires communication. Tomasello calls this form of interaction 'We-mode'. In the case of chimps hunting monkeys, however, while individuals are mutually responsive to one another's spatial position as they encircle the prey, each participant tries to maximize his *own* chance of catching the prey, without any prior joint goal or plan or assignment of roles. This is behaving in I-mode, not We-mode (60-63).

Children of even one year old, however, can work in We-mode. In a series of tests with 14-24 month-old infants the children collaborated easily in social games, but the chimps had no interest at all in the games and refused to take part in them. Researchers also engaged in collaborative activity with some very young children of about 18 months, and then exchanged roles the next time. The children easily adapted to their new roles, suggesting that they understood the adult's perspective and role. Chimps did not reverse roles in the same way, only having a first-person perspective. So, human collaborative activity is achieved through generalised roles potentially filled by anybody, including the self. This is the basis, together of course with language, of that unique feature of human culture, the institution. 'Social institutions are sets of behavioral practices governed by various kinds of mutually recognized norms and rules', which are concepts like 'mother's brother', or 'Prime Minister': 'no animal species other than humans has been observed to have anything even vaguely resembling [social institutions]' (xi-xii).

We are, then, innately social beings to whom rule-based co-operation comes quite naturally and this ease of collaboration and enforcement of norms is also closely connected with conformity:

> ...humans also have a tendency to imitate others in the group simply in order to be like them, that is, to conform (perhaps as an indicator of group identity). Moreover, they sometimes even invoke co-operatively agreed-upon social norms of conformity on others in the group, and their appeals to conformity are backed by various potential punishments or sanctions for those who resist. To our knowledge, no other primates collectively create and enforce group norms of conformity (xv).

The human passion for conformity, and readiness to punish those who violate it, should be obvious to everyone, (especially academics), as is our extreme sensitivity to our social reputations (consider here the blushing reflex), and our susceptibility to insult. There is also a corresponding need to live in a social world that 'makes sense', that is orderly and predictable; when a society's common values and common meanings are no longer understood or accepted, and new values and meanings have not developed, individuals find this very stressful. According to sociologists like Durkheim, among many others, such a society produces, in many of its members, psychological states characterised by a sense of futility, lack of purpose, and emotional emptiness and despair, and striving is considered useless, because there is no accepted definition of what is desirable. Studies of modern urban atomistic societies show repeatedly the lower levels of happiness and satisfaction that are typical. The human need for meaning and order as well as conformity is therefore a fundamental part of our nature which has important consequences for hostility between groups, as well as within them.

3. The other side of the coin

While there are very powerful tendencies in human nature that impel us to friendship, co-operation, and unselfishness, we now have to consider the limits to these, and what happens when these impulses are disappointed or members of 'our' group are threatened. The capacity for friendship also entails the capacity for hatred, while reciprocity, the universal desire and duty to return good for good, also entails the equally universal desire and duty to return bad for bad, and preferably something even worse. Revenge for personal injuries and slights is not just confined to ourselves, however, and is very easily generalised by friendship and the bonds of kinship to the impulse to take revenge for *their* injuries and slights as well. (I have myself lived in a society in Papua New Guinea dominated by revenge of this sort.)

If we were the selfish individualists that many biologists like Alexander suppose, and only able to co-operate with close relatives, the paradoxical result would be that any large-scale warfare would be impossible because, even if tribes or nations could somehow manage to develop, selfish individualists would run away rather than risk injury or death by fighting to defend them, unless their personal survival were immediately threatened. These biologists have therefore missed the essential point that warfare assumes *unselfish group loyalty*, and that the necessary result of solidarity within the social group must inevitably be at least *potential* hostility to outsiders: '...the best way to motivate people to collaborate and to think like a group is to identify an enemy and charge that "they" threaten us. The remarkable human capacity for co-operation therefore seems to have evolved mainly for interaction within the local group' (Tomasello 2009:100). Tomasello refers to the '...in-group, out-group mentality, which researchers have shown is operative even in very young infants (who, for example, prefer to interact with people who speak their own language even before they themselves speak' (94). 'A child's sympathetic habits, being formed in familial settings, may not extend much beyond these settings. We find it easiest to sympathise with people who are most like us, and may be most disposed to help those who are most like us'.[19] This propensity will be maximised in small-scale societies: 'Children reared in traditional rural sub-cultures and small semi-agricultural communal settlements co-operate more readily than do children reared in modern urban sub-cultures', and are also less competitive and more caring of others.[20]

Back in the nineteenth century, Herbert Spencer and Charles Darwin were quite familiar with this 'In-group/Out-group mentality' and both recognised what many modern biologists have forgotten: that human society necessarily involves both 'external self-defence and internal co-operation – external antagonism and internal friendship', which Spencer distinguished as 'the ethics of enmity' and 'the ethics of amity': 'As the ethics of enmity and the ethics of amity, thus arising in each society in response to external and internal conditions respectively, have to be simultaneously entertained, there is formed an assemblage of utterly inconsistent sentiments and ideas' (Spencer 1897:316). Spencer and Darwin both agreed that 'When two tribes of primeval man, living in the same country, came into competition, if (other circumstances being equal) the one tribe included a great number of courageous, sympathetic and faithful members, who were always ready to warn each other of danger, to aid and defend each other, this tribe would succeed better and conquer the other' (Darwin 1871:134).

It is a truism known to every politician, and one of the best supported conclusions of the social sciences, that the easiest way of increasing group solidarity is to invoke an external threat. A well-known experiment by Sherif and Sherif (1953) illustrates this very clearly.

They set up their investigation at a summer camp with 24 normal adolescent boys, who did not realise that they were taking part in an experiment, while the researchers also took great care to disguise themselves as camp staff. For the first three days, the boys were not divided into groups, but lived in one bunkhouse and were free to select their own bunks, seats at meals, friends for play activity, athletic teams, and so on. Quite naturally, leader-and-follower relations, and clusters of friendship relations began to develop, but these were cut short by the second stage of the experiment, when the boys were divided into two groups, red and blue, officially to allow them to carry out their preferred activities more easily.

The two groups were deliberately selected by the experimenters so that they should *not* be constituted on the basis of the informal friendship groupings that had already been established.

The aim of this stage was to keep the groups separated, and to develop the solidarity of each group without interfering with the freedom of the members to organise their own activities. These, which included swimming and camping, were carried out separately, and were designed so that a high level of co-operation was necessary for group success. Members of each group were invited to choose names for their group, the red group becoming the Red Devils, and the blue group becoming the Bull Dogs. In addition, 'Considerable group effort went into improving their cabins, stencilling insignia on T-shirts, making standards, signs, games equipment for the group etc. Both groups had private hide-outs which they worked collectively to improve...' (198).

As a result of these arrangements, hierarchical leadership patterns emerged, together with group praise and punishment, while group solidarity also became the basis for some antagonism to the other group. For example, three members of the Red Devils were branded as 'traitors' and even threatened until they saw less of the boys with whom they had been friendly in the first stage and who had subsequently become Bull Dogs. There was a general change in the pattern of friendship preferences, so that between 85 to 95 per cent of friendships were now within the groups, although there was no consistent enmity or hostility between the groups at this stage.

The next stage was designed to bring the two groups back into relations with each other that were competitive and mildly frustrating. Points were given not only for athletic events, but for excellence in performing camp duties as well, and the prize of a camping knife would be awarded to each member of the winning group. The point system was simple and clearly explained, but allowed some manipulation by the experimenters, so that for the first two days the two groups were given points that were fairly similar, in order to maintain the will to win on the part of both groups, and the groups were evenly matched in terms of size and skill.

While initially the two groups treated each other with good sportsmanship, as the competitive contest went on inter-group rivalry and hostility increased rapidly. This hostility was exacerbated by the failure of the Red Devils in the sports competition, a failure which they increasingly rationalised as due to cheating by the Bull Dogs (an unfounded belief). This friction and frustration was given further impetus by the final victory of the Bull Dogs and the distribution of the highly esteemed knives to them.

The experimenters then arranged a party in the mess hall ostensibly to reconcile the two groups, but in reality as a means of imposing further frustrations on the boys. Half the refreshments set out on the tables were battered and broken, as though damaged in transit, while the other half were undamaged and delicious. By a subterfuge the Red Devils were allowed to reach the mess hall first and told to help themselves, and naturally took all the best food to their tables. When the Bull Dogs arrived they were incensed by all this and hurled insults at the Red Devils, and the mess hall became the focus of further hostility at meal times with the Bull Dogs dumping dirty plates etc. on the Red Devils' tables, the Red Devils retaliating by dirtying the tables even more the next day, since it was the Bull Dogs' turn to clean the mess hall. Upon this the Bull Dogs retaliated by making the Red Devils' tables even messier, and they also hung up posters insulting the Red Devils.

At lunch relations deteriorated even further, until '...the groups were lined up against each other throwing waste material and food at each other'. Both sides were naturally convinced that the other side had started the fight. The staff intervened when the boys began throwing table knives and saucers at each other, and managed to stop the fight, but only with considerable effort. At this point it was decided to abandon the experiment, which in one sense had been almost too successful, and to break up the two groups by reintegrating them into a single camp-wide unit.

But despite the efforts of the counsellors to restore order and prevent further conflict, more battles, in which the boys pelted each other with green apples, broke out during the afternoon and the Red Devils planned and nearly carried out a night raid on the Bull Dogs.

This experiment provides a graphic illustration of the way in which the inherent co-operative tendency of human beings within groups is also an essential basis of conflict between groups – the ethics of amity and enmity. The Red Devils and the Bull Dogs were small groups of individuals who had not met before the experiment, but one of the striking features of human beings is our ability to extend the notion of 'us' almost without limit to complete strangers, because societies are not just groups of people, but also systems of ideas, so that vast numbers of people can think of themselves as bound together as brothers and sisters by nationality, ethnicity, social class, political ideology, or religion.

The following verses of the French National Anthem, the Marseillaise, were written in 1792, as the royalist armies of Prussia and Austria were about to invade France and crush the republican revolution. They push just about every button in the human psyche, and are an excellent illustration of how this intimate link between loyalty to the group and a corresponding hostility to outsiders, so well illustrated by the Fishers' experiment, can be hugely extended by political ideologies such as nationalism and republicanism:

Children of the Fatherland, let's go,
The day of glory has arrived!
Against us the bloody flag
of tyranny is raised
The bloody flag is raised!
In the countryside do you hear
These ferocious soldiers roaring?

They come right into your midst
To butcher your sons, your women-folk.

To arms, citizens,
Form your battalions,
Let us march, let us march!
So that their polluted blood
May drench our fields!

What does this horde of slaves,
Of traitors and plotting kings desire?
For whom are these vile chains,
These long prepared irons?
Frenchmen, for us, ah! what an insult!
What transports of fury it must arouse.
It is us they dare plan
To return to ancient slavery
(by restoring the Monarchy)

These words of the Marseillaise are a good reminder that emotions of solidarity and enmity can be generalised and extended very easily by ideas of brotherhood and fatherhood, taken from the family milieu to include whole nations, most of whom are complete strangers, and produce political ideologies that transcend nations entirely. Just as the Fatherland of France, and the revolutionary republican principles of Liberty, Equality, and Fraternity inspired frenzies of loyalty and hatred, of self-sacrifice in the cause, and murderous hostility to those who threaten it, longing 'to drench our fields in their polluted blood', so too the twentieth century showed the power of political ideologies based on race or the dictatorship of the proletariat and class hatred to produce massacres on a scale unprecedented in human history.

It is precisely because religious believers are as much

attached to their religions as people are to their countries, or to their political ideology, that the world religions have, on the one hand, the ability to bind together millions of members of many different races and nations, (something which atheists typically ignore), but that on the other their members can also react with violence and persecution towards those whom they perceive as external threats, or to those heretics who are seen as destroying internal solidarity, and are often more hated than external enemies. It is surely rather naive, then, to think that religion is uniquely prone to generate mass slaughter and violent persecution, rather than being just one among a number of such factors that also include politics, race, social class, language, and nationality. It was these, not religion, which produced the wars of the last century, the most violent in history, and the belief that if we removed religion we could remove the main cause of human conflict is clearly incorrect. Indeed, many wars in history have had nothing to do with group hatreds at all, but have simply been the result of kingly ambition and the desire for territory, power, and plunder. Religion has actually been calculated to have been the primary cause of only about 7 per cent of the wars in recorded history, half of which involved Islam (Day 2008:105).

4. Equality and hierarchy

Important emotional continuities between animals and Man exist, then, but ever since Darwin apes and monkeys have become especially symbolic figures in the human story, the scientific counterparts to Adam and Eve: biologists clearly relish the thought of our hairy primeval ancestors, archetypes of savagery, swinging through the trees, and we are supposed to have inherited their basic character-traits, however much we may try to disguise them by the trappings of so-called 'civilisation'. One of these traits is dominance and submission, or hierarchy. Dominance hierarchies are usually found, unsurprisingly, wherever animals live in groups and compete for food and mates (think of chickens, wolves, and horses), but biologists have been fixated on apes and monkeys because they think it is quite obvious that their dominance-hierarchies and alpha-males, in particular, can tell us something very special and profound about our own human nature. For example, after a long discussion of baboons, two sociobiologists conclude: 'Human political systems are based on hierarchy and competition for status... it must be understood that the process which gives rise to empire is *the very same process* [my italics] that primates engage in simply in order to exist and persist'.[21]

According to them, apes and monkeys can therefore provide us with the 'behavioural grammar' needed to understand human nature, especially power and domination. Among chimpanzees, 'dominance seems almost to be an end in itself for males of this species, and... alphas and other high-ranking individuals gain reproductive benefits via political intimidation in mating and food competition'.[22] Sociobiologists also think of power in very simplistic terms as mere bullying: 'The type of power I have in mind is straightforwardly conceived. In its raw form it is like the power we see exhibited in groups of chimpanzees... It is the dominant's power to intimidate and take something away from someone, or to force another to do something'.[23]

The problem for biologists who believe that we have simply inherited this lust for power and domination from our ape and monkey ancestors, is that ancient hunter-gatherers presumably resembled modern ones in being notably egalitarian, without any of the dominant alpha-males of the chimpanzee or baboon variety. (If any try to appear, they are rapidly put in their place.) Then, with the development of farming and more complex societies dominated by chiefs, kings, and emperors, dominance hierarchies appeared once again. One sociobiologist, Christopher Boehm, has tried to solve this apparent problem by arguing that hunter-gatherers are just as hierarchically disposed as chimpanzees, but have discovered how to act as a group to suppress potential alpha-male bullies, in what he calls a 'reverse-dominance hierarchy', which was then favoured by natural selection and became an inherited trait: 'It is primarily on the basis of vigilance that hunter-gatherers have kept their societies egalitarian in spite of individual tendencies that could lead to despotism. Over the long term, the result is a reverse social dominance... *with the subordinates firmly in charge.*'(my italics. Boehm 1999:88).

As a result, in modern democracies, too, we have the vote 'because we want to keep a say in our own governance, but, more basically, we exert it because we are suspicious of all governance and wish to limit the powers of those who lead and may therefore try to rule... Our earliest precursor, in this respect, may well have been an African ape living some 5 to 7 million years ago. This vanished ancestral hominoid was likely to have formed political coalitions that enabled the rank and file, those who otherwise would have been utterly subordinated, to whittle away at the powers of alpha individuals whose regular practice it was to bully them' (Boehm, vii).

While it is true that 'The three African great apes, with whom we share this rather recent [?] Common Ancestor, are notably hierarchical' (3), as are many social mammals, why should we assume that there is any significant continuity in this respect between apes and monkeys and our hunter-gatherer ancestors, let alone with us today? In the first place, when we are invited to speculate about the political lives of 'vanished ancestral hominoids', who disappeared 5 million years or so ago, and to 'develop a full behavioural portrait of the Common Ancestor of the four African-based hominoids [including us]' of 7 million years ago, we are entitled to some degree of scepticism. The leading biologist E.O.Wilson has pointed out that 'Two thousand generations, roughly the time since typical *Homo sapiens* invaded Europe, is enough time to create new species and to mould their anatomy and behaviour in major ways'.[24] But 5 million years gives *250,000* generations (at 20 years to the generation) which is more than 100 times as many generations as those necessary to create new species, while 7 million years gives 350,000 generations. (Baboons, indeed, are not apes at all but monkeys, and the split between these and apes occurred no less than 25 million years, or 1,250,000 generations ago!) Given these enormous evolutionary distances, how would 'a full behavioural portrait' of the Common Ancestor be possible, and what relevance would it have anyway?

Modern humans, as found among hunter-gatherers, are clearly an entirely new species with a number of unique characteristics which set them quite apart from the world of apes and monkeys, in particular through their enormously enhanced cognitive and co-operative abilities:

- The modern human brain with all its formidable cognitive and imaginative powers.
- The possession of language, with profound implications for social life, such as planning, social bonding, giving information about other group members, and conveying values and social norms.
- The possession of tools and weapons that could be used for killing other people as well as animals, and therefore bad news for bullies.
- The control of fire and the cooking of food (see below).
- None of the primate competition for mates, but stable, recognised unions between males and females. The elimination of female estrus allowed frequent sexual activity that cemented this pair bonding, and also 'reduced the potential for [male] competition and safeguarded the alliances of hunter males' (Wilson 2004:140-41).
- Marriage as an economic as well as a sexual relationship. Women cook food for their husbands, who provide meat and protect wives and their food (Wrangham 2012).

- None of the primate competition for food, but co-operation in hunting and systematic rules for sharing.
- A unique repertoire of behaviours such as crying with tears, disgust, and laughter.
- A long period of children's dependence on parents and adults.

These vast differences between human and primate society radically change the rules of social life from individualistic competition to group co-operation, in which the dominance hierarchies of the baboon and chimpanzee type would be quite out of place.

So the biologists' fixation on the social life of apes and monkeys, far from illuminating the basics of human nature, only serves to confuse the issue. They are guilty, in particular, of a very basic fallacy when they suppose that human social hierarchies are the same kind of thing as the dominance hierarchies of apes and monkeys. The fallacy is this: the bullying by alpha-male chimpanzees, biting, scratching, jumping up and down and screaming and waving branches, is *entirely self-serving*, with minimal concern for the welfare of the group, and is simply part of the ongoing competition between all the males for food and mates. But human social leadership and positions of authority have nothing to do with bullying of the chimpanzee variety: the notion of a leader imposing his will on his followers like an alpha-male chimpanzee misses the whole point of leadership in simple societies, which is that the leader has to attract people by having something to offer them, by being a social benefactor in some way, not by threatening them, because individuals are free to live more or less where and with whom they like, and have free access to all the necessities of life. The idea that the strongest man could simply seize control and bully all the rest of the group into submission is quite unrealistic: even the strongest man has to sleep, the other men are just as well armed, and even if such a would-be dictator were not murdered, people would simply abandon him and go and live somewhere else.

Positions of power and leadership in human societies are produced by situations in which some people control what other people want or need, like food, land, personal security, political skills, status, wealth, the favour of the gods, professional expertise, knowledge, and so on. In other words, power requires *dependency*, and among hunter-gatherers there is precious little of that, because social organisation is very simple and everyone has equal access to resources. This is why leadership roles are so muted in their type of society, not because we have inherited 'a reverse-dominance hierarchy'. In the more complex societies produced by agriculture and the domestication of animals, people may cease to be self-sufficient in defence, or in access to resources or to the supernatural, or a host of other things, so they will be willing to accept inequality of power because they obviously get something out of war-leaders, or clan heads, or priests. Once we understand that human social hierarchies are based on dependency, not on bullying, and are generally regarded as quite *legitimate* and in the general interest, Boehm's claim that 'One of the great mysteries of social evolution is the transition from egalitarian to hierarchical society'[25] ceases to be a mystery at all, but a non-problem produced by the delusion that humans are still really apes at heart.

The New Guinea Big Man, for example, gains his status primarily as an organiser of feasts and dances in which his own group competes with others, and as a public orator on such occasions. He attracts followers by his force of personality and his political skills as an organiser and diplomat in dealings with other groups, and can certainly behave despotically to those at the bottom of society, the 'rubbish-men'. But while he obviously enjoys his status, he is accepted and regarded as a legitimate leader because he is seen as an essential asset by his group of followers, and in my experience tends to be gracious and polite.

It is clear that human beings have evolved a unique ability to co-operate within the we-group, which is very ancient, and this is completely incompatible with any conflicting and equally powerful urge to dominate one another in the very crude manner depicted by Boehm. If we are looking for some basic feature of human nature that would facilitate our ready acceptance of hierarchical relations we should avoid speculation about chimpanzees or baboons, and need look no further than the human family, and those long-drawn-out parent-child relations which are centred on dependency. All that happens as societies become more complex is that the opportunities for dependency become more frequent, and that we generalise our ingrained attitudes to the authority of parents and elders to include Big Men, clan heads, nobles, and so on, ending with kings who are fathers of their people, and priests who are fathers of their flocks.

Once this is understood, we can see that the social hierarchies of increasingly complex societies like chiefdoms, kingdoms, empires, and modern industrial society have nothing in common with the individualistic bullying of chimpanzee groups but are the result of complex systems of dependency, and are essential for organising large-scale societies. In formal hierarchical organisa-tions people have to take orders, but all can recognise that this is necessary for the greater good of the organisation and the wider society. So the captain of a warship in Nelson's navy, reading the Articles of War to his assembled ship's company, that gave him the power of life and death and flogging over all of them, was not remotely comparable to an alpha-male chimpanzee throwing rocks. Captains were respected as essential to the functioning of the ship, and some, like Nelson himself, were revered by their crews.

On the other hand, where people are in these dependent relationships with leaders, what they do expect is *reciprocity* – competence, good order, justice, generosity, concern and so on – and if they do not get it then social dominance does indeed become regarded as a form of bullying, and revolution and mutiny are often the result. The current discontent across the Western world with politicians and bankers is a good example of this. So it is generally obvious that hierarchical social organisation offers serious temptations to bullying and arrogance; history is filled with cases of rulers and those in positions of power who have abused their authority, and the same remains true today of all hierarchical organisations in business, politics, and in the rest of society. As Abraham Lincoln said, if you really want to test a person's character, give them power.

Again, human societies are uniquely different from any animal group because they are based on ideas, on symbolic culture, and as they become more complex, differences of status emerge that have nothing to do with physical strength or aggression, but become associated instead with wealth, descent, education, social class and aristocracy, and a wide range of personal achievements and symbolic attributes that are quite distinct from power itself, and can have no possible counterpart in the purely material world of animals. For example, political leaders in traditional societies are typically legitimated by their aristocratic descent, and by their religious status, but these concepts cannot have the slightest meaning for animals. So while human individuals compete in terms of their status, these status differences are not simply individual differences, like those of strength and aggression as found among apes and monkeys, but are part of a social hierarchy that can have no parallel in any animal group. (We come back to societies as systems of ideas in §7.)

5. Consciousness and free will

If biologists' treatment of human nature is significantly flawed, their claims about Man become especially contentious when we move on to consider consciousness and free will. Since it would appear impossible to feel emotions or pain without being conscious, we can assume that a wide range of animals share many aspects of consciousness with us, though probably not self-awareness, while rational thought itself seems to require language. We regard our inner mental life of experience, of consciousness, thoughts, feelings, and perceptions as distinct from our bodies, however closely linked to them. But the idea of the mind as having its own reality has always been an affront to materialists. According to the famous Behaviourist psychologist B.F.Skinner, for example, it is a pre-scientific fantasy: 'Where are these feelings and states of mind? Of what stuff are they made? The traditional answer is that they are located in a world of non-physical dimensions called the mind and that they are mental. But another question then arises: How can a mental event cause or be caused by a physical one?'[26] Obviously, says Skinner, it can't because this would be miraculous, and modern believers in an inner mental life are as absurd as primitive animists, who supposed that physical objects could be inhabited by spirits. The only solution to such nonsense is to dismiss the whole idea of the mind, consciousness, thought, and the superstitious belief in free will and human dignity, and instead 'follow the path taken by physics and biology by turning directly to the relation between behaviour and the environment and neglecting supposed mediating states of mind'.[27]

Modern biologists entirely agree with Skinner. Although the development of computers helped make Behaviourist theory itself obsolete, because they seemed to show how internal 'states of mind' could actually be recreated in electrical devices, they amply supported Skinner's fundamentalist materialism: 'The rise of computers and, in their wake, modern cognitive science, completed the conceptual unification of the mental and physical worlds by showing how physical systems can embody infor-mation and meaning'[28], so that the world of the mind has been transported into 'the scientifically analysable landscape of causation'. As the biologist and co-discoverer of DNA, Francis

Crick, graphically expressed it: 'You, your joys and sorrows, your memories and your ambitions, your sense of personal identity and free will, are in fact nothing more than the behaviour of a vast assembly of nerve cells and their associated molecules... This hypothesis is so alien to the ideas of most people alive today that it can truly be called astonishing'.[29]

The emergence of human beings is therefore only a continuation of the earlier evolution of the universe, and its physical, chemical, and biological processes, and not in any way different or discontinuous from what has preceded it.

> In this vast landscape of causation, it is now possible to locate "Man's place in nature" to use Huxley's famous phrase, and therefore to understand for the first time what humankind is and why we have the characteristics that we do... Human minds, human behavior, human artifacts, and human culture are all biological phenomena – aspects of the phenotypes of humans and their relationships with one another.[30]

These claims that the existence of the computer finally solves the mind-body problem are obviously very wide of the mark, however. Charles Babbage showed back in the nineteenth century with his mathematical engines that sets of gear-wheels could carry out advanced cognitive tasks: it only requires us to design machines to operate according to strict rules that we lay down. The computer is no different in principle from Babbage's engines, except that it uses electricity and switches instead of gears, and so has rather more superficial resemblance to the human brain, because that, too, uses electricity. But the computer is no more 'thinking' or 'conscious' than the telephone wires when they are transmitting a human conversation, the 'speak-your-weight' machine when it weighs us, or a book that is 'full' of deep thoughts. The telephone wires only carry electrical impulses, the weighing machine only has levers and wheels, and the book only has marks on its pages, which convey information because we have specifically coded them to do so. We can easily use our conscious minds to design physical systems 'to embody information and meaning' because we put it in there: the real problem is how consciousness could develop spontaneously in a purely material brain *without* anyone to put it there. While it may be hard to imagine how a mental event could cause a physical one, we shall see that it is equally hard to explain how physical events in the brain could cause mathematics, for example. Indeed, consciousness has become known as 'the Hard Problem'.

While neurologists can now trace in some detail the physical pathways and processes in our nervous system and brain by which we feel pain, see colours, and hear sounds, they are no closer to knowing what pain actually *is*, or why light in a certain part of the spectrum gives us the distinctive sensation of redness, why concordant sound-waves should also be pleasing to our ears, and, indeed, what consciousness itself is, of how it can be generated by trillions of sub-atomic particles. According to Dawkins, 'Human thoughts and emotions *emerge* from exceedingly complex interconnections of physical entities within the brain' (Dawkins 2006:14). But 'emerge' as used by Dawkins here is a mere word, with no more explanatory value than 'Hey Presto' when used by a magician pulling a rabbit out of a hat.[31]

Regardless of anything the neuroscientist may say, we know from our own personal experience that human consciousness and culture form a world that is entirely different from the physical world: unlike physical objects, ideas do not exist in time, they have no size or weight, motion or position in space, and they do not cause each other like physical events. Value, meaning, truth, and logical implication can have no meaning at all in the physical world, but only when organised in human culture and in human consciousness and personality. So, too, there is a whole realm of the imagination in art, music, literature, and science, and a range of social ideas like person, promise, trust, loyalty, and morality in which personal interaction between minds is fundamental. Religious experience, too, has its own very characteristic features, especially those of a mystical nature, which we shall take up in the next chapter. The natural sciences, however, can take no account of personal experience, as the mathematical physicist John Polkinghorne observes:

> Science is principally concerned to explore only one dimension of the human encounter with reality, essentially that which can be called impersonal, open to the unproblematic repetition of the same phenomena, irrespective of the place of investigation or the character of the investigator... Science's declining to engage with the personal dimension of experience implies the limited character of the account which it can give of reality.[32]

Scientists, nevertheless, typically contrast individual experience to scientific evidence as 'subjective' to 'objective', in which 'subjective' more or less means 'false', and 'objective' means 'true'. This ignores the obvious fact that scientists themselves depend on their individual experience of experiments to acquire their knowledge of the physical world. They also assume that each of them is the same person conducting an experiment as he was yesterday or last week, but Professor Susan Blackmore, like many other philosophers, neurologists, and biologists, regards the very idea of the self as an illusion: '...every time I seem to exist, this is just a temporary fiction and not the same "me" who seemed to exist a moment before, or last week, or last year'.[33] Who, then, is the author of her various books and why should we believe anything 'she' says?

Far from being illusions, therefore, consciousness, a sense of self, and that traditional philosophical bogey-man, 'free will', are not only the basis of ordinary sensation and the decisions of daily life, but are necessary for reason, mathematics, and science itself. Indeed, if consciousness and everything associated with it were mere illusions or shadows of reality, without the power actually to do anything, why would they have evolved at all, and what adaptive value could they possibly have?

Furthermore, if electro-chemical processes in the brain are the actual causes of our conscious thoughts, which are mere by-products or shadows of these underlying physical processes, then this would also destroy the claim of logic and mathematics, and therefore scientific reasoning in general, to be objectively true, because physical processes, as such, can be neither true nor false, logical or illogical. (Being the square root of something is not a physical property.) So if there is an unbroken chain of purely physical causes in the brain that produce logical and mathematical thought, where can our belief in logical necessity and proof come from? By what chemical processes known to science can organic molecules and ion flows generate mathe-matical theorems? As an illustration of this: Suppose we take a simple proposition like 'If two things are equal to a third thing, then it is logically necessary that they are also equal to each other'. If we accept that a thing can only have a single value at any one time, then we can see why the proposition must be true by supposing the contrary, that they might be unequal to each other. But if A and B, despite equalling C, had different values (e.g. if A=2, B=3), this would also require C to have two different values (2 and 3) simultaneously, and this in turn would be a contradiction. We are therefore convinced that the initial propo-sition *must* be logically valid; but if this sense of logical proof, and the arguments that led to it were merely produced by the movements of physical particles in the brain, and the electrical connections between certain synapses, the whole basis of their objective truth and logical necessity would disappear, and they would become like any other physical process – the wind blowing in the trees or the raindrops running down the windowpane.

Underlying the logical necessity of the proposition we have been discussing there must be conscious thought, in the first place – there can be no such thing as unconscious logic, any more than there can be unconscious pain. But there must also be free will, in the sense that such decisions as 'This is logically valid', or 'This is logically false' must be taken purely on the logical merits of the case, uninfluenced by any non-logical factors, such as the state of one's brain. This applies to the whole of logic and mathematics, and therefore to the validity of natural science in general.

Indeed, the whole argument that we cannot make free rational choices is self-contradictory:

> Your affirmation of the view, 'there are no such things as free choices' itself presupposes at least one free choice. Thus to argue for the view that there are no free choices is self-defeating. Basically, this argument is saying that all knowledge and enquiry presupposes choice: we choose between alternatives in making any kind of judgement. Even the judgement that there are no free choices, if such we make, entails a choice on rational grounds. If Determinism is true, then there is no such thing as rational judgement, only predetermined courses of action.[34]

It is therefore astonishing that many highly intelligent people like the biologist Crick, philosophers like Dennett and Ryle, and psychologists like Skinner and Blackmore, can manage to persuade themselves that their own consciousness, their own experience, is an illusion. As a contemporary philosopher has commented, '...this particular denial is the strangest theory that has ever happened in the whole history of thought, not just the whole history of philosophy' (Strawson 2006:5). He points out that while we have direct knowledge of our own consciousness, our scientific knowledge of the physical world is actually of a very restricted and indirect nature. As Bertrand Russell said:

Physics is mathematical not because we know so much about the physical world but because we know so little: it is only its mathematical properties we can discover. For the rest, our knowledge is negative... The physical world is only known as regards certain abstract features of its space-time structure – features which, because of their abstractness, do not suffice to show whether the physical world is, or is not, different in intrinsic character from the world of mind.[35]

So attempting to reduce consciousness and experience to what science knows of the physical world is trying to explain the better known by the very much lesser known. If, however, we accepted the possibility that consciousness could be an attribute of a much more sophisticated type of matter than our current understanding of it, then thought could be an integral part of the universe. No one knows if this is actually the case, and the more traditional argument has been for a dualistic universe of mind and matter[36], but whatever is the truth about the ultimate nature of matter, mind cannot be argued away in the manner of Crick and others as a mere by-product of the kind of 'matter' that is currently known to science. A reasonable view of the cosmos has to accept that it contains more than the fundamental particles and the basic forces presently known to physics.

A further fundamental problem with the claim that all mental processes are nothing more than bio-chemical processes in the brain is that our mental processes have been proved to explain some of the structure of matter. Bio-chemical processes might just conceivably produce poetry, which does not have to be literally true – 'The moon doth with delight look round her when the heavens are bare'. But what possible connection could there be between the biological organisation of our brains and the deep structure of the physical universe, as revealed in equations like $E=mc^2$, which bring together such fundamental concepts of the universe as energy, mass, and the velocity of light, and are wholly outside ordinary experience, and are also true? As Einstein said, 'The most incomprehensible thing about the universe is that it is comprehensible'. In the words of Polkinghorne:

> Of course, evolutionary survival necessity can be expected to have moulded our brains so as to make them able to make sense of the world of everyday experience. However, our human ability to understand the subatomic quantum world, totally different in character from the macroscopic world of everyday happenings and requiring counter-intuitive ways of thinking for its understanding, is another matter altogether. That subatomic world has no directly discernible impact on human experience and to regard its intelligibility to us as simply the result of a happy spin-off from mundane survival necessity is a highly implausible suggestion.[37]

It is indeed, and anthropologists know that the thought of primitive societies is rather more notable for magic than anything remotely resembling science: we saw earlier that mathematical ability, in particular, could not have been selected for in human prehistory. Polkinghorne continues:

> And the mystery is deeper even than that, for it has turned out that it is mathematics – that most abstract of disciplines – which time and again has provided the key to unlocking the secrets of the physical universe. It is an actual technique of discovery in fundamental physics to seek theories that are expressed in terms of equations possessing the unmistakeable character of mathematical beauty, a property which the mathematically minded can readily recognise and agree about. It involves such qualities as economy, elegance and what mathematicians call 'being deep', by which they mean that extensive consequences are found to flow from seemingly simple initial definitions, as when the endless

baroque complexities of the Mandelbrot set are seen to derive from a specification that can be written down in a few lines. This heuristic strategy is no mere act of aesthetic indulgence on the part of physicists, for 300 years of enquiry have shown that it is just such mathematically beautiful theories that prove to have the long-term fertility of explanation that convinces us that they are indeed describing aspects of the ways things are. In other words, some of the most beautiful patterns that the mathematicians can think about in their studies are found actually to be present in the structure of the physical world around us.[38]

Professor Roger Penrose emphasises the reality of mathematical structures, and that they are not simply the arbitrary products of human imagination:

How 'real' are the objects of the mathematician's world? From one point of view it seems that there can be nothing real about them at all. Mathematical objects are just concepts; they are the mental idealizations that mathematicians make, often stimulated by the appearance and seeming order of aspects of the world about us, but mental idealizations nevertheless. Can they be other than mere arbitrary constructions of the human mind? At the same time there often does appear to be some profound reality about these mathematical concepts, going quite beyond the mental deliberations of any particular mathematician. It is as though human thought is, instead, being guided towards some external truth – a truth which has a reality of its own, and which is revealed only partially to any one of us.

The Mandelbrot set provides a striking example. Its wonderfully elaborate structure was not the invention of any one person, nor was it the design of a team of mathematicians... It would seem that this structure is not just part of our minds, but has a reality of its own. Whichever mathematician or computer buff chooses to examine the set, approximations to the *same* fundamental mathematical structure will be found... The computer is being used in essentially the same way that the experimental physicist uses a piece of experimental apparatus to explore the structure of the physical world. The Mandelbrot set is not an invention of the human mind: it was a discovery. Like Mount Everest, the Mandelbrot set is just *there!*[39]

Ironically, therefore, it is precisely this extraordinary success of mathematics and the physical sciences which makes the conventional materialist theory of the mind seem increasingly implausible, and is actually more consistent with the suggestion that thought is part of the universe, which makes sense at some deep level. In this context the old idea that it is governed by a unified body of rational laws given by a divine source of order is not absurd, and we shall return to it in the next chapter.

Setting pure reason aside, why, for that matter, should we find beauty in so many aspects of the natural world and its design? What selective advantage is there in the human aesthetic sense, and why should we be so moved by great music and art? As an anthropologist, therefore, it seems to me that while we have obviously evolved from pre-human animal forms, the attempts by evolutionary psychologists to show that the human mind is *merely* a set of adaptations by hunter-gatherers to the conditions of East Africa during the Pleistocene are not supported by serious evidence. The further project to assimilate the whole of human culture and thought into the purely physical realm of biology and chemistry, in my view goes beyond science altogether, and derives instead from a cult of philosophical materialism.

6. Societies are systems of ideas

Here we move from individual behaviour, motives, and thought to the societies and cultures that individuals construct, and these are not just groups of people, but systems of ideas. While we have a genetically-based human nature, we can only become functioning human beings by growing up surrounded by other human beings in a society, and absorbing its culture – its ideas, knowledge, beliefs, values, and institutions. Human culture was actually as radical an innovation in the history of the world as the emergence of life from non-living matter. By 'culture' I do not mean simply learning new behaviour and passing it down the generations, which many animal groups can do. I mean the ability to use language to transmit ideas – knowledge, values, customs, and social institutions – to other people. The origin of language is one of the most obscure and debated problems in human evolution, but however and whenever it began, once it had developed, it allowed human beings to be linked together not just by purely animal relations such as mutual grooming, or sharing the same odours, but by shared ideas and institutions.

Human society is therefore a new kind of system altogether because its institutions exist in people's heads as ideas, but which are also public ideas communicated by language: one cannot *see* the Prime Minister, for example, but only a man, and someone who does not know what being a Prime Minister *means* has to be told. This can only be done properly by explaining how his role fits into the British Constitution, which in turn involves explaining cabinet government, the rule of law, democracy, and so on. Our whole society, then – the nation, the government, money and the banking system, trades unions, companies, local councils, and so on – forms a world of ideas, a landscape, within which people have to interact with each other, and which power-fully affects their behaviour. Furthermore, as we can see in the case of the Prime Minister and the British Constitution, these ideas form *systems* which have their own laws and properties.

We know quite well that, to take some elementary examples, in differently designed traffic systems exactly the same population of drivers may either experience a series of accidents and jams, or freely flowing traffic; for exactly the same population of voters, a first-past-the-post electoral system will give a very different outcome from a system based on proportional representation; while national economies are typically subject to booms and slumps which are outside the control, and often the comprehension, of any individuals. Political systems, financial systems and electoral systems are systems of *ideas*, as well as of individuals, and these systems clearly have their own dynamics and laws of operation which are distinct from the motives of the individuals who compose them.

The suggestion that societies are systems of ideas is, however, anathema to Darwinists, who detest both systems and ideas, and regard everything in human society and culture as produced by the biological motivations of *individuals*, trying to maximise their inclusive fitness. According to E.O.Wilson, the founder of sociobiology, '...cultures are not superorganisms that evolve by their own dynamics. Rather, cultural change is the statistical product of the separate behavioral responses of large numbers of human beings who cope as best they can with social existence'.[40] Biologists, therefore, regard human societies not as systems, but as nothing more than *populations* of individuals. Wilson is trying to theorise well outside his zone of expertise: not only is his idea of human society and culture completely contradicted by the whole of economics, political science, sociology, and anthropology, but biologists are compelled to admit that they have to take culture into account as well.

As Richard Dawkins has conceded, 'These [genetic] ideas... [alone] ...do not begin to square up to the formidable challenge of explaining culture, cultural evolution, and the immense differences between human cultures around the world...'.[41] He is one of a number to propose that the gene itself is just one example of the more general category of a *replicator*, a unit of information or instruction that can make copies of itself and which can be passed on in some way, and that another example of a replicator is the 'meme'. This is anything in human culture that can be imitated – an idea, a tune, a dress fashion, and so on – and like the gene has the sole 'purpose' of replication, of making copies of itself. The main point here, then, is that culture is being treated as nothing more than a *population* of memes all competing with each other, just as a society is nothing more than a *population* of competing human individuals.[42]

It is not widely understood, therefore, that Darwinism is not just a fairly straightforward theory of biological evolution – 'proving that we are descended from monkeys, not Adam and Eve', as the popular image has it – but has far grander ambitions. It is committed to what is known as Universal Darwinism: this claims that matter is all that there is in the universe; that humanity must be included in the natural sciences; that design, and purpose in general are all illusions, and, indeed, that the laws of physics have themselves evolved by natural selection. Not only is there no God or Supreme Being of any kind, but human culture, thought, consciousness, purpose, and free will are also illusions, to be completely explained by the variation and selection of memes in the same manner as genes. Universal Darwinism is therefore 'a scheme for creating Design out of Chaos without the aid of Mind' (Dennett 1995:50), and that includes human minds as well as the Divine Mind. Dennett has described this theory as a 'universal acid', which 'eats through just about every traditional concept, and leaves in its wake a revolutionized world-view...' (63).

It might be objected that *human* design seems to have played a fairly obvious part in the evolution of agriculture, the early state, writing, and the Industrial Revolution, to name a few major examples. Darwinists argue, however, that just as societies are merely populations of competing individuals, cultures are merely populations of competing *memes*, which, as I have said, are anything in human culture that can be imitated. The mindless meme, like the gene, has the sole 'purpose' of replication, of making copies of itself, while memes themselves are based on physical brain states inside the heads of the individuals. The evolution of culture is therefore nothing more than changes in the relative frequencies of competing memes inside people's heads, so that, like God, our consciousness is also an illusion, created by the memes themselves. While memeticists don't deny that conscious states, like our individual identity, *seem* to exist, they are illusions created by the memes in our brains, because memeticists cannot admit that they are directed by conscious human goal-seeking; this would allow the demon of the designer to reappear on the scene, which would be almost as bad as the return of God.[43]

So if we are told that we do not really take an aspirin to cure our headache, but that the 'aspirin for headache' meme has actually been using us like a parasite to replicate itself, there is no point in criticising this as bizarre, since the memeticist would take it as a compliment, that only goes to show what a revolutionary insight is provided by 'the meme's eye view'.

Even the creative process is to be explained by the blind combination and competition of memes in our brains:

> I have suggested that human consciousness is not the driving force behind the creation of language (or anything else for that matter) ...In discussions about creativity people often assume that consciousness is somehow responsible for creativity, but their view meets with serious problems as soon as you try to imagine what it means. You are almost forced into adopting a dualist position, with consciousness as something separate from the brain, that magically leaps in and invents things... Human brains and minds are a combined product of genes and memes. As Dennett (1991:107) puts it 'a human mind is

itself an artefact created when memes restructure a human brain in order to make it a better habitat for memes' ...All this is a wonderful example of replication creating design out of nowhere. As ever, there is no designer other than the evolutionary process (Blackmore 1999:206-7).

Since Blackmore is particularly keen to combat 'false' memes, notably those of religion ('a virus of the mind'), and the illusion of personal identity, she is obliged to admit that 'Memes do not need to be true to be successful' (180). She concedes that it is to the memes' advantage to be able to mimic truth, just as it is to their advantage to be able to mimic other successful memes like 'altruism', 'successful', 'scientific', and so on. This, however, is fatal to the whole memeticist case, because if the only 'aim' of memes is to replicate as much as possible, there is no reason why they should have any innate bias towards truth or anything else of concern to human beings. As Dennett says, 'The first rule of memes, as for genes, is that replication is not necessarily for the good of anything; replicators flourish that are good at... replication – for whatever reason!' (Dennett 1995:362)

So how can we tell when memes are only mimicking the truth? As Blackmore has ruled out the operation of conscious reasoning as a means to attain truth, there can only be the mindless competition of the memes inside the 'meme habitat' of our brains, and so there is no way left by which any objective notion of truth could be established, and *this includes the theory of memetics itself*. Indeed, if culture is simply this mindless competition of swarms of memes in our brains, without the intervention of consciousness and reason, there is simply no objective basis on which science and truth themselves could be established. Dennett's 'universal acid' therefore dissolves the whole of science, with all other forms of truth, and instead of 'a revolutionised world-view' merely leaves universal nonsense.

Memetics, like behaviourism, also removes the possibility of free will: 'The self is not the initiator of actions, it does not "have" consciousness, and it does not "do" the deliberating. There is no truth in the idea of an inner self inside my body that controls the body and is conscious. Since this is false, so is the idea of my conscious self having free will' (Blackmore 1999:237). So if I give some money to a homeless person, this is not really my choice, but the 'give money to a homeless person' meme replicating itself in my brain, and if I decide to mug an old lady instead, this is not me either but simply the 'mug an old lady' meme at work too. The whole idea of human moral agency, of responsibility, principles, and purpose therefore becomes completely meaningless.

The Nobel Prize-winning biologist, François Jacob, warns against the tendency to abuse a general theory such as natural selection in the manner that Dennett, Dawkins, Blackmore, and many others have done in the case of the meme:

A theory as powerful as Darwin's could hardly escape misuse... [T]he very success of the theory of natural selection in accounting for the evolution of the living world made it tempting to generalize the argument and shape it to explain any change at all occurring in the world. Similar systems of selection have thus been invoked to describe any kind of evolution, whether cosmological, chemical, cultural, ideological, or social. Such attempts, however, appear to be doomed to failure from the start, for natural selection represents the outcome of specific constraints imposed on every single living organism. It corresponds, therefore, to a mechanism fitting that particular level of complexity. The rules of the game differ at each level. New principles have to be worked out at each level.[44]

7. Conclusions

From the fact that the earth is an ordinary planet revolving around an average star, which is one of billions in the outer reaches of our galaxy, and that Man evolved only in the last instants of geological time, out of the same stock that produced chimpanzees and gorillas, it has been fashionable to conclude that, contrary to the traditional view that Man is of central importance in the scheme of things, we have no significance at all. But, in the first place, 'significance' here must obviously be a purely human judgement, since the mindless physical universe can form no opinion of our importance one way or another. Moreover, the anthropologist is also struck by the 'scientific' criteria chosen to demonstrate our insignificance: to be small, weak, recent, peripheral, and of low birth are actually the traditional criteria of insignificance that we find in primitive societies and the ancient world. The scientific mind should conclude, on the contrary, that since organisms of human complexity require a large number of prior, and improbable, conditions to be in place, and therefore a long evolutionary process, it is only to be expected that the universe must be both huge and of immense age to allow a being such as Man sufficient time to develop. Our ability to understand the universe and ourselves should be of incomparably greater significance, at least to intelligent beings, than our physical location in the universe, or the length of time we have been around, or our ancestry.

It has also been noted for some time that the evolution of life itself was only possible because a number of basic physical constants of the universe happen to have exactly the right values. If any of these had been slightly different, life would have been impossible, and while this certainly does not prove in any way that the universe must therefore have been set up with *us* in mind, it adds further support to the idea that the development of life and mind could be integral parts of its design.[45] And when one considers the extraordinary marvels of human achievement in music, painting, sculpture, literature, architecture, mathematics, and science, and the fact that in Man, the material universe can finally understand itself, the proposition that we are just a pointless evolutionary accident seems far from compelling.

It is perfectly reasonable to apply science to the study of Man – that, after all, is the basic aim of anthropology in all its branches – as long as we realise that there are some major differences between the social and the natural sciences. But although the various biological theories of Man claim to be based on rigorous and impartial science, in many respects they derive from a World-View, an ideology that is not scientifically neutral at all, but desperately wants to 'unmask' what is perceived to be human self-importance, and to overthrow the traditional understanding of Man and his place in nature, that has been held by all the great civilisations of the world, and show that he is essentially an ape instead. But the theory that baboons and chimpanzees can give us a unique insight into how power works in human societies is based on a very crude model of animal behaviour which contributes nothing to political science; the claim of inclusive fitness theory about fundamental human selfishness, and that we can only behave altruistically to our relatives has subsequently been revised, and is also contradicted by numerous studies of human behaviour; evolutionary psychology is largely an imaginative enterprise, based mainly on speculation about unknowable events in the Pleistocene in East Africa; natural selection is an entirely inappropriate model for explaining social evolution and its extreme version, memetics, like Universal Darwinism itself, far from being based on reason and evidence, has been discredited by the extreme vagueness of the meme concept itself, its failure to solve any actual problems, and the fact that by denying the role of human consciousness and reason it destroys the basis of science itself.

Biological theories of Man are also based on a philosophy, a

metaphysical materialism, that is intensely hostile to the importance of ideas and to thought in general, which is regarded as
virtually the same as the supernatural, and to all forms of
consciousness, purpose and meaning. I do not think it is unreasonable or rhetorical exaggeration, to say that the materialist
views of Man we have been examining have a deeply anti-human
bias, although usually cloaked in a Humanist veil of tolerant
liberalism. It is notable that prominent Humanists, such as
Grayling and Kurtz, in their attacks on religion as cruel and
inhuman (which it certainly can be) entirely avoid all the anti-
human implications of modern evolutionary biology, and it is a
theme taken up again in Chapter 3 on Humanism.

Materialists who claim that natural science is the *only* genuine
form of knowledge, and can answer all the ultimate questions
about the meaning of life, why we are here, and why the universe
and its laws are as they are forget that the success of science was
achieved at a price. This was the abandonment in the seventeenth
century of anything like Plato's and Aristotle's attempts to answer
these ultimate 'why?' questions, as being outside the practical
scope of science, which can only be concerned with 'what
happens' and 'how'. As Sir Peter Medawar said,

> That there is indeed a limit upon science is made very likely
> by the existence of questions that science cannot answer and
> that no conceivable advance would empower it to answer.
> These are the questions that children ask – the 'ultimate
> questions' of Karl Popper. I have in mind such questions as:
>   How did everything begin?
>   What are we all here for?
>   What is the point of living?
> Doctrinaire positivism – now something of a period piece –
> dismissed all such questions as non-questions or pseudo-
> questions such as only simpletons ask and only charlatans of
> one kind or another profess to be able to answer. This

peremptory dismissal leaves one empty and dissatisfied because the questions make sense to those who ask them, and the answers, to those who try to give them; but whatever else may be in dispute, it would be universally agreed that it is not to science that we should look for answers.[46]

The scientist, when speaking strictly as a scientist, should therefore accept its necessary limitations and consider the existence of God, or some kind of Supreme Being, as outside the scope of science, whatever his or her private convictions may be. Dawkins claims that 'the existence of God is a scientific hypothesis like any other'[47], but a scientific hypothesis must be testable, and it can only be tested if it is clear and unambiguous. The 'God' of Dawkins, however, turns out to be notably vague and very far from testable: 'I am not attacking *any particular version of God or gods* [my italics]. I am attacking God, all gods, anything and everything supernatural, wherever and whenever they have been or will be invented'.[48]

Chapter 2

Religion and Morality

Many religious believers, of various faiths, hold the simple-minded view that morality can only be based on God's commandments: murder, stealing, lying, and adultery, for example, are wrong because God says they are in the Bible, or the Koran, or some other scripture so that without God there could be no moral rules at all. Protestants, in particular, have maintained this, although many others including Nietzsche and Sartre have also believed that if God disappears from the picture then it's a free-for-all and all hell breaks loose, or that we each have to make up our own moral code as we go along, which comes to much the same thing. But this clearly won't do because if murder, stealing, and lying are only wrong because God has forbidden them, they would automatically become good if He changed His mind about them. Trying to base moral precepts on the authority of God alone therefore deprives them of any independent status, and calling God good also becomes meaningless, since *whatever* God might be or command would necessarily be good – mere power worship, in other words. Many believers, therefore, have always realised, at least since Plato, that God actually condemns murder, stealing, lying, and adultery *because* they are wrong independently of His will, and this has long been the position of the Catholic Church for example. But if this is so, how did we discover the difference between right and wrong in the first place?

1. The social basis of our moral ideas

The obvious answer is that we get this knowledge from our experience of social life: we could not call God just and merciful, for example, unless we already knew what justice and mercy *meant* in terms of the actual behaviour of people in our lives and our society. More than two thousand years ago Aristotle defined Man as a social animal, and said that the good life for Man was *eudaimonia,* 'happiness' or 'flourishing'. Just as fish need water, so we need society to become human and we saw in the first chapter that humans are naturally sociable and co-operative, as well as competitive. For us even to survive childhood every society must be based on parental care, and some degree of co-operation and mutual assistance. So it is hardly surprising that even in the simplest societies we find some rules about the proper behaviour concerning parents and children, sex and marriage, property and theft, sharing and reciprocity, fairness, revenge and violence, and respect and insult, and the appropriate sorts of behaviour towards men, women, old people and children, and so on. As societies become more complex, and kings emerge, it is generally expected that they have a duty to maintain law and order, to administer justice and prevent the strong preying on the weak such as widows and orphans, to be victorious in battle, and to give their people prosperity.

These moral rules in turn rest on those basic emotional aspects of human nature[1], of 'amity and enmity', that we discussed in the previous chapter: '...morality involves strong convictions. These convictions don't – or rather can't – come about through a cool rationality: they require caring about others and powerful 'gut feelings' about right and wrong'.[2] Basic moral codes, 'the common decencies', will therefore be found in every society, including hunter-gatherers and simple farming tribes, not because they have been divinely revealed, but because they are necessary to carry on any social life at all. Again, personal qualities such as courage, toughness, hard work, generosity, good temper, and intelligence are generally admired, although given varying emphasis in different societies, while people everywhere would be in broad agreement about what constitutes benefit and harm, a good deed and a bad one.

Despite the great variability of values across cultures it is therefore the essential features of human nature and the requirements of social life that are the basis of ethics. This is why we find that murder and robbery are condemned in societies all over the world which have never heard of the Ten Commandments, and why 'thief' and 'liar' are insults in any language. And it is for these reasons that we can dismiss the sillier forms of moral relativism that some anthropologists and philosophers like to play with.[3] In Macaulay's words:

> Every human being, be he idolater, Mahometan, Jew, Papist, Socinian, Deist, or Atheist, naturally loves life, shrinks from pain, desires comforts which can be enjoyed only in communities where property is secure. To be murdered, to be tortured, to be robbed, to be sold into slavery, to be exposed to the outrages of foreign banditti calling themselves patriots, these are evidently evils from which men of every religion, and men of no religion, wish to be protected; and therefore it will hardly be disputed that men of every religion, and of no religion, have thus far a common interest in being well governed.[4]

But if the problems of government and social control were the limits of ethics, one may well ask why we need to bring religion into the matter at all: surely we can work out the basic principles of how to be good neighbours and what is a tolerable society to live in without asking for help from the Almighty? But matters are not that simple. With the rise in the ancient world of cities, markets and money, international trade, the huge expansion of material wealth and luxury, and of ever greater social inequality, with aristocrats and poor peasants, slavery, powerful rulers and armed conquest of neighbouring peoples, a whole new range of moral challenges appeared that went far beyond the elementary issues of murder, theft, and vengeance with which people had to cope in earlier societies and the simple requirements of law and kingship, and involve a more profound view of the world.

Are power and wealth and luxury and sexual indulgence the best things to be aimed for in life, or is virtue more important than the satisfaction of mere bodily desires or social ambition? What are the characteristics of the truly noble or virtuous person? What is a human being? Why do we have to be moral? What's wrong with eating people or having sexual relations with animals? Do we have any obligations to foreigners? How should we treat people we have conquered? Can they be killed or exploited without mercy and enslaved? How are social inequalities and kingship to be justified? What do the rich and powerful owe to the poorest and weakest in society? Do their lives have any value at all? Must we always obey the commands of our kings or is there some higher law by which they themselves are to be judged? If other societies have different moral ideas from ours why do we think ours are the best and most natural? Which is the more reliable guide to how we should act; our traditional customs or some higher and more universal standards? What is the secret of happiness and what is the point of living anyway?

These fundamental problems about the human condition are of roughly three types. The first are about human nature and raise questions like: what is the basis of happiness – material pleasure or virtue? What is virtue? Are we basically selfish or altruistic? Do we have free will? Are intentions morally relevant? Do we have a higher spiritual and a lower physical nature? The second are about the relation of the individual to society: Is altruism naive? Should we only bother about members of our own society or do our obligations extend to foreigners, and if so, why? Are moral values relative to each society or are they universal? What is the difference between law and morality? Do individuals have rights that are in some way prior to society or does the social order have its own special moral value? And the third type of problems are about the relation of Man and society to the universe and the natural world: Do we have a special status or are we just another species of animal? What counts as being human – are foetuses, imbeciles, or people with Alzheimer's really human, for example? Is there such a thing as human dignity? Does the universe have a basic meaning and a moral dimension or is it basically nothing but senseless matter?

These are profound questions about the human condition and the meaning of life, and the answers to them need more than our experience of living in society and the basic dictates of human nature and seem to require a broader and subtler world-view. According to atheists there are basically just two ways of finding the answers to such questions. One is religion, based on 'faith', which Dawkins has defined as 'blind trust, in the absence of evidence, even in the teeth of evidence' in the existence of super-natural beings – basically "God".[5] The other is a non-religious approach, which A.C.Grayling calls '...a naturalistic world-view, that is, a view to the effect that what exists is the realm of nature, describable by natural laws. This is accordingly a world-view premised on observation, reason and science, and excludes any kind of faith-involving element, and specifically excludes belief in or invocation of [supernatural beings]'[6], or as Robert Park has put it, more concisely, 'Science is the only way of knowing – everything else is just superstition'.[7]

2. Faith or reason?

But do we in fact have a simple choice between faith and science? First of all, 'faith', in the sense of 'beliefs that seem plausible but we are unable to verify' is not peculiar to religion. For example, as Aldous Huxley said, 'Science and technology could not exist unless we had faith in the reliability of the universe – unless, in Clerk Maxwell's words, we implicitly believed that the book of Nature is really a book and not a magazine, a coherent work of art and not a hodge-podge of mutually unrelated snippets'.[8]

Atheists also take it for granted that all beliefs, religious or otherwise, must be based on evidence. This sounds quite reasonable until we realise that 'evidence', in the scientific sense, has a special meaning: it has to be publicly accessible, like the temperature shown on a thermometer which we can all see; it has to be testable to check if it is accurate; and it has to be repeatable as in the case of experiments. These are what make evidence 'objective' for the purposes of the natural sciences, and very properly so, but evidence in this sense is highly specialised and completely rules out the personal, subjective *experience* which each of us has and constantly uses to understand the world. As Keith Ward says:

> Whereas it seems plausible to require that evidence must put factual claims beyond reasonable doubt, that is not true of many personal experiences. There can be vivid and trans-forming personal experiences of immense significance which are not accessible to others, and which can change a person's whole view of the world without providing anything like universal certainty. Those who insist upon the sole sufficiency of scientific method are forced to ignore the most important testimony available to human persons, the testimony of personal experience that can only be known by introspection.[9]

We saw earlier that the scientific dismissal of experience could not be justified, and even the distinction between experience and evidence is not as rock-solid as it might appear. Many people familiar with classical music, for example, consider that Beethoven's later quartets are particularly beautiful. Others might dismiss them as horrible scraping, yet those who are deeply moved by them could say that their beauty is objectively present in the music and that some people simply can't appreciate it. But there is no way of proving or disproving the objectivity of beauty in music or in anything else by scientific experiment.

Our most important judgements about life, therefore, are

based on personal experience, not just on 'evidence', so the idea that there are only two types of explanation – those based on faith and those based on science – is wholly implausible. There is a vast range of political, economic, and ethical problems, for example, which the physical sciences cannot even attempt to solve by experiment and measurement, but where nevertheless people's opinions are based on experience, which is much more than blind trust with no regard for reason or facts. In the same way, we shall find that the 'truth' of religion has far more resemblance to human experience and to questions of politics and ethics than to laboratory experiments and to hypotheses in the natural sciences.

Secondly, we are asked to accept the plainly incorrect statement that reason has no place in religion. The atheists' image of religion seems primarily derived from modern Christian and Muslim fundamentalists. These religions have ancient roots, and it has pleased atheists to present Christianity, via its Old Testament roots, as a form of Bronze Age religion, put together by desert goat-herders whose primitive idea of God has remained basically the same ever since. This entirely fails to grasp the development of the philosophical aspect of religion from the time of the ancient Greeks, Indians, and Chinese, and that intellectual theories of the divine have evolved out of all recognition from their ancient origins. In the Middle Ages, for example, St. Thomas Aquinas (1225-1274) proposed five arguments for the existence of God, and we can take that from Possibility and Necessity as an example of what they look like:

- We find in nature things that are possible to be and not to be, that come into being and go out of being i.e., contingent beings.
- Assume that every being is a contingent being.
- For each contingent being, there is a time it does not exist.
- Therefore it is impossible for these always to exist.

- Therefore there could have been a time when no things existed.
- Therefore at that time there would have been nothing to bring the currently existing contingent beings into existence.
- Therefore, nothing would be in existence now.
- We have reached an absurd result from assuming that every being is a contingent being.
- Therefore not every being is a contingent being.
- Therefore some being exists of its own necessity, and does not receive its existence from another being, but rather causes them. This all men speak of as God.

Or again, St Anselm, Archbishop of Canterbury (1033-1109), produced what came to be known as the Ontological argument for the existence of God, as follows: 'God, by definition, is a being than which *no greater* can be conceived. God exists in our understanding. If God exists in our understanding, we could imagine Him to be greater by existing in *reality*. Therefore, God must exist.' Aquinas disapproved of this argument, but later philosophers took it more seriously, notably Descartes and Leibniz, and in the twentieth century the leading logician Kurt Gödel developed it further. I am not claiming that any of these arguments actually proves the existence of God but am merely showing that the level of reasoning involved is far beyond 'blind trust, in the absence of evidence, even in the teeth of evidence', and even further beyond the thought processes of Bronze Age goat-herders.

Aristotle, in particular, has been particularly influential on Western thought, and the fact that his philosophy, with its emphasis on the fundamental importance of reason, was absorbed into Catholic Christianity by St Thomas Aquinas in the Middle Ages should caution those who still think that religion is nothing more than blind trust and has nothing to do with reason or philosophy. (Indeed, Aquinas is often criticised for placing too much emphasis on reason.) Philosophical arguments for the existence of God have been of no interest, however, to ordinary believers, for whom religion has always been a matter of social practice and personal experience, but in this sense, too, religion has evolved fundamentally in the course of history, as we shall now see.

3. The evolution of religion

Victorian evolutionists were deeply interested in the prehistoric origins of religion: one of the most eminent, Sir Edward Tylor, believed that it originated with the idea of the soul (from the experience of dreams in particular) subsequently developing into notions of spirits and gods and he therefore defined the essence of religion as 'belief in Spiritual Beings'.[10] Tylor was one of the earliest social anthropologists, and in the light of all the world-wide research since his day this notion of religion now seems crude and simplistic, which is probably why it appeals to modern atheists. I shall explain in a moment why I think it needs substantial revision, but we first need to consider a very common theory of why people found the idea of spiritual beings attractive.

(a) *Religion as a crutch*
One of the favourite explanations for belief in supernatural beings has been that our cavemen ancestors needed to evolve some sort of intellectual 'security blanket' to protect them from the fear of predators and other threats, and that modern religion is a survival of this evolutionary defence mechanism.

But if the function of supernatural beliefs has been to give us intellectual comfort, then the human race has generally gone about this in a very odd way, since the terrors of the supernatural have been at least as obvious as its consolations. Belief in evil spirits is universal, and the deities of hunter-gatherers and early farmers, for example, far from being comforting father-figures as

Freud supposed are generally punitive, arbitrary, and thoroughly nasty, much more concerned with punishing offences against taboos than with rewarding or helping people. Much the same could be said of the wrathful Yahweh of the Old Testament, or the terrifying figures of Kali and Shiva in Hinduism, all representing death and destruction as well as creation and renewal; the powers of evil in general, notably the Devil, are conspicuous features in all the world religions. 'The Spirit is not necessarily friendly or universally benevolent. It is often seen as a force of fertility and power which is indifferent to moral concerns and which can be used for the dominance of one tribe over others'.[11]

Fears of witchcraft, the evil eye, and a great deal of magic have also blighted the lives of millions, and witchcraft is a belief that is particularly difficult to explain by any kind of wishful thinking. While it may be satisfying to have someone to blame for *particular* misfortunes, one also has to live with the general fear of what the witches are going to do next. This, and the problem of detecting those thought to be responsible for all this imaginary malevolence have permeated many societies with an odour of fear and suspicion that is neither comforting nor functional.

Again, the belief that the soul survives death is pretty well universal, but if it is just the product of wishful thinking, why has the after-life been represented in most societies (until the rise of the world religions) as generally a gloomy place, where the dead endure a sad existence and envy all the joys of the living? And, once the idea of some kinds of rewards and punishments after death developed in the world religions, why have the punishments been so important? If, for example, the Christian idea of Heaven was merely the product of wishful thinking, of 'pie in the sky when you die', why (at least until the modern era of Father Christmas and the Easter Bunny) did most Christians fear they might not get there at all and were in serious danger of Hell fire instead? It was not entirely without reason that the ancient Epicureans claimed that by denying the existence of the gods (or at least their power to do anything) they were relieving mankind of a burden that made them miserable.

Belief in an afterlife, too, is often explained by the emotional need to be reunited with one's loved ones after death, or to go to a place of compensation for the sufferings of this life. Such hopes may appeal to modern Westerners, but they do not figure very prominently in other cultures and earlier epochs. A happy reunion with one's loved ones in the next world is not, strangely enough, a hope that anthropologists usually come across when they study primitive societies. What really interests the members of such societies is not if their departed relatives and ancestors are happy in the next world but *if they are angry with the living* – have we honoured our ancestors' bones with a sufficiently lavish dance, or sacrificed an ox of suitable size, or broken a taboo such as marrying someone from the wrong clan? The general impression given by the anthropological evidence is that primitive peoples do not believe in the afterlife because it fills an emotional need (either for personal survival or reunion with loved ones), but simply because it seems an obvious fact, based on the experience of dreams in which they think they meet the dead, on ghostly apparitions, and on out-of-body experiences.

(b) *Early religion*
It is essential to be clear from the outset that religion is much broader and more complex than a simple psychological process (belief in supernatural beings) which has persisted essentially unchanged throughout the ages from cave to cathedral. To explain the origin of the idea of God, some biologists have proposed that the brain has a special 'agent-detection' mechanism, leading us to invent personal beings who cause particular types of event, and that there might even be a 'God gene'. In the early stages of the development of thought people certainly think most easily about causes as the actions of some

kind of agent, so there is no doubt that supernatural beings are a very important aspect of religion at all levels of development. But when anthropologists encounter religion even in the primitive societies of hunter-gatherers and early farmers, they find it is far wider in scope than supernatural beings. One has the impression, however, that atheists do not feel obliged to engage in a scholarly discussion about the nature of religion. According to Dawkins, for example, 'The notion that religion is a proper *field*, in which someone might claim *expertise*' is like claiming to be a 'fairyologist'[12], being apparently unaware that 'religious studies' are a perfectly respectable subject in the social sciences.

The exclusive emphasis on belief in spiritual beings can be seriously misleading in the study of primitive religion especially because it downplays the equal importance of notions of cosmic order, and their expression in symbolism and ritual – religion as giving *meaning* to human experience of the world. I would therefore add Robert Bellah's definition of religion as 'a set of symbolic forms and acts that relate Man to the ultimate conditions of his existence'[13], and Keith Ward's view that 'Religions can differ greatly from one another, but a central, if not absolutely universal, theme is the existence of a supernatural realm in relation to which some form of human fulfilment can be found'.[14] The nature of that realm, and what forms that fulfilment takes have changed very much, however, in the course of history.

Members of hunter-gathering and farming societies assume they can interact by words and actions with the physical world *as if it were part of their own social world*, and this is the really important point about the early forms of religion. They are not focused on a Heavenly world quite different from the world of ordinary experience. As Bellah puts it, 'They are concerned with the maintenance of personal, social, and cosmic harmony and with attaining specific goods – rain, harvest, children, health – as men have always been'.[15] It is also often impossible to draw a clear distinction between the religious and the social. So clans in tribal society may not be seen merely as social institutions but are often thought of as having a close, 'totemic', relationship with species of birds, animals, and plants, and their founders and heads are seen as endowed with sacred powers. Authority is peculiarly liable to attract sacred status, so that in the traditional society of the Tauade of Papua New Guinea, when a Big Man died his body would be put into a specially built enclosure which women were not allowed to enter. Pigs were then slaughtered inside the enclosure and the sacred bull-roarer was whirled, away from the gaze of the women. If enough boys were available they would be kept inside the enclosure in a little hut for several months where they could imbibe the vitality of the dead chief and were taught by adult men to be tough and aggressive. The Big Man's corpse, meanwhile, had been put on a special platform in his hamlet where it was allowed to rot, and it was thought that people absorbed the powers of the Big Man in the smell. Big Men also had a special association with certain birds of prey and sacred oaks, and were believed to be essential for the general health and well-being of the group.

Again, when I lived with the Konso of Ethiopia they told me that their very complex age-grading system, which governed the relations between the generations, made the crops grow. By this they meant that when there was harmony in society then the Sky/Rain God Waqa, and the Earth, which also had a moral power, would cause their fields to flourish. I would therefore agree again with William James that 'If any one phrase could gather [religion's] universal message, that phrase would be "All is *not* vanity in this Universe, whatever the appearances may suggest"'.[16] That is, the world around us and our place in it make sense in some deep fashion that is also essential for our well-being.

Notions of cosmic order are fundamental because they provide the meaningful context, the stage, on which the various supernatural beings perform, a mythological and poetic world-view that takes account of how things began and of how we fit into the wider cosmos, and the forces of life, fate, birth and death. A good example of this is the so-called 'Dreamtime' of the Australian Aborigines:

> The mythological era... is regarded as setting a precedent for all human behaviour from that time on. It was the period when patterns of living were established, and laws laid down for human beings to follow. This was the past, the sacred past; but it was not the past in the sense of something that is over and done with. The creative beings who lived on earth at that time did perform certain actions then, and will not repeat them: but their influence is still present, and can be drawn on by people who repeat those actions in the appropriate way, or perform others about which they left instructions. This attitude is summarized in the expression 'the Eternal Dreamtime', which underlies the belief that the mythological past is vital and relevant in the present, and in the future. In one sense the past is still here, in the present, and is part of the future as well.[17]

All over the world in myth and ritual we find a range of symbolic categories that link the social and the natural worlds: the wild and the tame; order and disorder; purity and pollution; normal and abnormal; village and bush; life and death; male and female; right and left; symbolic reversal; light and dark; and sky and earth. These are not primarily concerned with supernatural *agents* as such, but serve to embed human society in what we would call the natural world, and all such categories are expressed by a rich symbolism in ritual and myth. (It is for these reasons that religion has always had profound associations with art.) But this intermingling of society and nature also necessarily introduces some form of consciousness and personality, and therefore beings of some sort, into nature, because these are also integral to our experience of social relationships. As Keith Ward says,

> ...*personalisation is not an attempt to explain the occurrence of events* [my italics]. It is rather an attempt to enter into certain sorts of personal relations with natural powers – relationships of awe, reverence, gratitude and, yes, intercession. This is not a scientific hypothesis, but the adoption of a basic reactive attitude to the natural powers that surround us, and of which we are part.[18]

The notion of the *sacred* actually captures these ideas much more satisfactorily than that of 'religion', with its inevitable modern institutional associations of churches, bibles, and creeds, which give a totally inaccurate and misleading picture of primitive religion.

In modern Western society we also take it for granted that religion is centred on beliefs, on doctrines such as the Trinity and that the activities involved are something other-worldly which happen in churches, and are quite different from banks and hospitals, factories, offices, and all the practical activities of daily life. But this is our own peculiar view of religion and gives an entirely misleading view of its history. Unlike the church services with which we are familiar in which individual salvation is the central objective, primitive religion is entirely about the practical well-being of the community. Its rituals do not have creeds and doctrines nor do they involve personal spiritual experience, such as prayer or meditation, nor the well-being of the soul, a subject which tends to attract little interest or discussion beyond the fact that it is the element of the person that survives death and joins the ancestors. Supernatural beings may therefore play little or no part in ritual which can be described as a kind of public magic, the communal manipulation of sacred objects and actions to bring Life and prosperity to the *group*. (The idea that magic is quite different from religion, central to Frazer's *Golden Bough*, is really a Protestant idea that originated in the Reformation.)

In ritual, the settled life of the village, in particular, acquires great symbolic importance as the basis of the civilised and the tame, and the opposite of the wild bush and forest, the abode of those non-human and *impersonal* forces of creation and destruction that also play a great part in religion. The changing seasons and activities of the agricultural year, especially sowing and harvest, have an obvious and powerful resonance for religion because they are the basis of the ritual cycle that is devoted to securing Life in all its forms. The Earth often has a special significance in agricultural societies where it may take on the guise of Woman in whom the seed is sown. We may also find that, opposed to the Earth, is the Sky, the source of the rain that is so essential for the crops, and the Sky is often represented as male, impregnating the Earth.

Blood sacrifice became an almost universal ritual in tribal societies with domesticated animals and the basic idea seems to be that the shedding of animal, and especially human, blood is an act of power. It could be used for different purposes, the commonest being as expiations for sin – often some sort of offence against the sacred order rather than a crime – or to promote life and fertility. As ideas of the gods became more elaborated sacrifice was often seen as a work of strengthening them: 'The gods, as the forces of nature, were the source of all life and sustenance, but they depended on the energy that human beings returned to them in the form of sacrifices'.[19] It was the special duty of ancient kings to perform the most important sacrifices to sustain the gods of the sun, rain, plants and animals on which their people's prosperity depended.

Gods and other supernatural beings are therefore more important as beings of power, bringers of Life and Death, and guardians of cosmic order, rather than as moral agents, but if they do punish sins such as lying, oath-breaking, theft and murder, they do it in this life and not the next. Broadly speaking, this divine retribution indicates a need for people to believe that their most important intuitions about their society and values are not just arbitrary, made-up social conventions, but are somehow rooted in reality, are 'part of nature'. So, for example, Truth, in the sense of honesty and integrity is a central social value for the Konso and the fact that Waqa, the Sky god, is seen as punishing oath-breakers with death is not just a useful social sanction but is also a guarantee of its absolute value in the scheme of things which in later civilisation became known as the law of nature.

Just as ideas of the soul are vague there is hardly any psychological exploration of the inner self and its complexities. Although people obviously have some awareness of the motives and intentions of others, in primitive societies they may not distinguish, for example, between accidental and deliberate homicide and they think of inner states as basically inaccessible: vengeance and punishment are based on what a person has actually done rather than on any investigation of why he did it. They also have little idea of the conscience as a kind of inner voice that prompts us to do right and avoid evil; the notion of 'conscience', like that of romantic love, is not something that springs spontaneously and universally from every human breast but has to be developed in the right social circumstances. The justifications given in primitive societies for behaving morally are not based on the voice of conscience, but the fear of social condemnation and ridicule and losing one's good name and reputation. Probably for similar reasons there are no moral heroes who rebel against social norms in the name of higher principles. While belief in some sort of after-life is universal people generally have little interest in its details and the general attitude is that prosperity in this world is what matters. There is little or no idea of punishment in the after-life for evil deeds and rewards for good, though in some cultures chiefs and heroes are supposed to get privileged treatment in the next world. The most important aspects of primitive deities are therefore as sources of power and fertility and the flourishing of corporate, social life but this view of them was to change radically during the first millennium BC.

The reader will have detected many features of the Old Testament in this description of primitive and archaic religion. For example Yahweh, the God of Israel, was clearly understood originally simply as a tribal god of battle, one among many, and worshipped by blood-sacrifice, not the much later Universal Creator portrayed in Genesis. Quite apart from containing many other primitive features, we must realise that the Old Testament is the account of a whole society and its extremely bloody history of struggle with its neighbours, about *politics*, therefore, and the attempts of various leaders to create a society of a higher moral and religious type among a brutal and obstinate people at a fairly primitive level of cultural development. Invoking an angry and punitive God, who demanded exclusive allegiance and would take no nonsense from anyone who disobeyed may have been the only way in which they could get their message across. On the other hand, it is also important to note that the Babylonian exile had profound spiritual consequences and the moral ideas described in the Old Testament show considerable development, especially in the teachings of the prophets and the Wisdom literature.[20] When we come to the society in the time of Jesus and His disciples, however, we enter a very different world, where politics has become completely separate from religion, and Jesus could be a teacher of personal morality and individual salvation.

(c) *The emergence of the world religions*
During the middle of the first millennium BC people in China, India, Iran, and the Mediterranean world experienced a great deal of social turmoil: large-scale use of iron and other techno-logical innovations, increased international trade, commer-

cialism and the appearance of money, rapid urbanisation and enormous increases in wealth and luxury for the upper classes, together with the rise of empires, warfare, conquest, and political instability, all in various ways eroded traditional values and social bonds. This produced confusion and even despair, when educated people questioned the whole meaning of life and tried to find the secret of happiness and tranquillity of mind. The great expansion of wealth and luxury and social inequality also provided wonderful new opportunities for pride, greed, envy, wrath, lust, gluttony, and sloth that had been much more restricted in simpler societies.

Religion now underwent a profound revolution, and it was in these new circumstances that what we know as the world religions began to emerge among the literate classes of the towns. Far from this religion being produced by desert goat-herders, or even peasants, 'it was the townsman who was much more likely to be numbered among the devout'.[21] This period has been called the Axial or Pivotal Age because, in the cities especially, it led to a new breed of thinkers and religious teachers who took the lead in trying to solve these problems which were as much philo-sophical as religious. The philosophers and religious teachers of the Axial Age, and later of Christianity and Islam, were funda-mentally concerned with the question 'What is happiness or well-being and how does a person achieve it?' Debate became normal, and the experience of argument and the need to give rational justifications of one's opinions to counter one's opponents were major factors in making people, really for the first time in history, consciously aware of their own mental processes. Popular opinion or traditional authority are no longer treated as the obvious and only guides to proper conduct, and there is a new opposition between conventional opinion and the critical views of an intellectual elite of experts, prophets, or sages. The claims of conscience in the face of social pressure to conform become more clearly recognised.

This 'discovery of the mind'[22] had profound implications for the new moral awareness of the self and for developing ideas of the soul. It was also crucial, as we shall see, in creating the idea of Man as a thinking being, which gave him a unique status in the cosmos. Thinkers in these civilisations were searching for a more transcendent and universal authority on how one should live that went beyond the limits of their own society and traditions, and beyond the purely material prosperity and success that was the focus of tribal religion. 'Everywhere one notices attempts to introduce greater purity, greater justice, greater perfection *and a more universal explanation of things*'.[23] They not only thought about society and the nature of Man in a new way, but also about the traditional gods.

A good example of the new attitude is the Greek Xenophanes (c.545 BC), who said: 'Homer and Hesiod have attributed to the gods everything that brings shame and reproach among men: theft, adultery, and fraud... Mortal men imagine that gods are begotten, and that they have human dress and speech and shape... If oxen or horses or lions had hands to draw with and to make works of art with as men do, then horses would draw the form of gods like horses, oxen like oxen...' Instead of this naively human image of the gods, said Xenophanes, 'One god there is... in no way like mortal creatures either in bodily form or in the thought of his mind... effectively, he wields all things by the thought of his mind.'

In Greece this became the idea that the cosmos is governed by a rational principle, *logos*, a kind of inherent self-ordering property, so that it forms a purposeful whole whose parts and processes are not just interrelated but comprehensible to Man as a thinking being. Since intellect and reason are uniquely human and set us apart from the animals, we have the very important idea that the essential and distinctive mental element in human beings, the soul, is akin to the creative and ordering element in the cosmos, of Man as microcosm in relation to the macrocosm.

This profound doctrine takes us far beyond the crude formu-
lation of the gods as beings who punish and reward human
actions: it is a transition from Power to Wisdom, and is the real
point of contact between the human and the divine in the
transcendent systems of ethics that were formulated by the world
religions. Ideas similar to the Logos appear in the concepts of
Bráhman in India, Hokhma or Wisdom in the Old Testament, and
Tao in China, which were both universal and also linked to the
soul of every individual. Leibniz was later to call this 'the
perennial philosophy', found in all the world religions: '...the
metaphysic that recognizes a divine Reality substantial to the
world of things and lives and minds; the psychology that finds in
the soul something similar to, or even identical with, Divine
reality; the ethic that places man's final end in the knowledge of
the immanent and transcendent Ground of all being...'.[24] In the
New Testament, the Logos concept was synthesised with the
creative Word of God and the Wisdom of the Old Testament,
notably at the beginning of St John's Gospel, where the Logos
'...became particularly significant in Christian writings and
doctrines to describe or define the role of Jesus Christ as the
principle of God active in the creation and the continuous struc-
turing of the cosmos, and in revealing the divine plan of salvation
to man'.[25] It really needs to be strongly emphasised that
Christianity was the heir to Greek thought, particularly Plato and
Aristotle, as well as that of the Hebrews, a fact that is typically
ignored or even denied by Humanists.

The Stoics took this idea of Logos further than any others. It
came to mean the rational order of the universe, an immanent
natural law, a life-giving force hidden within things and a power
working from above on the sensible world, so that in Stoic
teaching the whole natural order also came to be identified with
the providential will of Zeus. Man has his proper place in the
scheme of things, which if he is wise he will try to comprehend
and so live in accordance with his true nature.

Stoicism asserted that Man and God (or the gods) are rational beings, and that because all Men are sons of God and because of this common attribute of reason, all Men, of whatever race or social status, slave or free, are equal. (This egalitarianism of the Stoic philosophy was reflected in St Paul's conception of a universal Church "Where there is neither Greek nor Jew, circumcision or uncircumcision, Barbarian, Scythian, bond nor free" [Paul came from Tarsus, a centre of Stoic teaching.] Moreover, since ...the Stoics deemed the only qualification necessary for citizenship to be wisdom, all Men the world over and without distinction are capable of attaining this status by developing their rational faculties. Thus is the concept of citizenship opened up to universal application. However, a good citizen must obey the law. That indeed is tautologous; but what law is a citizen of the world to obey? The Stoic answer was 'the law of nature', a code consisting of fundamental principles of justice emanating from divine reason and discernible by Man through the exercise of that same faculty.[26]

The basic idea was not therefore that we are special *simply because we are cleverer than the animals* but because the cosmos is itself governed by the same reason as exists in us, which therefore unites us and what we may call 'God' in a unique way. This was also the necessary basis of a new universalism binding the whole human race, the idea that all human beings have mutual duties of consideration to one another. The idea of Natural Law was subsequently to be of great importance in European thought, and in the Middle Ages Aquinas incorporated it into his system of moral philosophy. But we should also note that beyond these aspects of Wisdom, Reason, and Law, the divine comes to be thought of, especially in Christianity but in other traditions too, as embodying universal Love for mankind, and that this is another way in which the world religions differ from earlier forms. We shall come back in more detail to the profound impact of Divine Love on human moral systems, and here I only wish to correct the perhaps overly-philosophical image of the divine that may have been given so far.

Corresponding to the spiritual view of the cosmos in the Axial Age is a general rejection of material and worldly values. We find 'the emergence in the first millennium BC all across the Old World, at least in centres of high culture, of the phenomenon of religious rejection of the world characterized by an extremely negative evaluation of Man and society and the exaltation of another realm of reality as alone true and infinitely valuable'[27], although Israel was a major exception here. This radical distinction between the spiritual and the material stresses the inferiority of the body to the mind and especially the soul: 'Devaluation of the empirical world and the empirical self highlights the conception of a responsible self, a core self, or a true self, deeper than the flux of everyday experience, facing a reality over against itself, a reality which has a consistency belied by the fluctuations of mere sensory impressions'.[28]

The soul now came to be seen not as some crude vital essence but as the highest, sometimes the most intellectual part of the person, whose moral perfection is the route to salvation whereas the physical body is the source of hindrances to perfection – lust, gluttony, sloth, and greed, for example – because physical temptations are immediate and powerful obstacles to doing what is right, and powerful reinforcements of self-centredness. Denial of what we would call the ego through asceticism is therefore an essential element in all the world religions. In Buddhism, Hinduism, Taoism, and later in Christianity the highest path of all was withdrawal from the world entirely into an ascetic life of the hermit or monk.

All over the ancient world, then, it was believed that the soul was not only immortal but actually shared in the divine, so its aim was union with the divine after death as the soul was liberated from its material existence. As Socrates, for example, was about to drink the hemlock that would end his life because he refused to flee from his city as a matter of principle, Plato records him as telling his followers:

> There is one way, then, in which a man can be free from all anxiety about the fate of his soul – if in life he has abandoned bodily pleasures and adornments, as foreign to his purpose and likely to do more harm than good, and has devoted himself to the pleasures of acquiring knowledge, and so by decking his soul not with a borrowed beauty but with its own – with self-control, and goodness, and courage, and liberality, and truth – has fitted himself to await his journey to the next world (*Phaedo*, 115a).

The death of Socrates relates not only to asceticism but to the more general theme of the moral hero who sacrifices everything for his principles or for other people. In the words of William James,

> In heroism, we feel, life's supreme mystery is hidden. We tolerate no one who has no capacity whatever for it in any direction. On the other hand, no matter what a man's frailties otherwise may be, if he is willing to risk death, and still more if he suffer it heroically, in the service he has chosen, the fact consecrates him for ever. Inferior to ourselves in this or that way, if yet we cling to life, and he is able to "fling it away like a flower" as caring nothing for it, we feel him in the deepest way our born superior.[29]

As Jesus said, 'He that loveth his life shall lose it; and he that hateth his life in this world shall keep it unto life eternal' and 'greater love hath no man than this, that he lay down his life for his friends'.[30] The whole struggle to do the right thing, to keep to one's principles, to love others, inevitably pits the sincere believer against the temptations of physical pleasure, wealth, social prestige, and success, 'the world, the flesh, and the devil', and is a basic theme of all the world religions and their moral values. The world religions therefore made it their business to come to terms with a world in which all was *not* well. In the words of William James,

> ...since the evil facts are as genuine parts of nature as the good ones, the philosophic presumption should be that they have some rational significance, and that systematic healthy-mindedness, failing as it does to accord to sorrow, pain, and death any positive and active attention whatever, is formally less complete than systems that try at least to include these elements in their scope. The completest religions would therefore seem to be those in which the pessimistic elements are best developed. Buddhism, of course, and Christianity are the best known to us of these. They are essentially religions of deliverance: the man must die to an unreal life before he can be born into the real life.[31]

These developments in the idea of the soul were also marked by a very significant change in religious experience. From the most ancient times it seems that a variety of techniques, such as hallu-cinogenic plants, drumming, and dancing, had been used by shamans to produce trance states in curing rituals, while dreams and vision quests relating to supernatural beings are also reported in many tribal cultures. While all these techniques for producing altered states of consciousness persisted and have continued into modern society, the growing awareness of the inner self was also accompanied, in all the major religions, by new sorts of spiritual exercises in which the divine is approached by meditation and prayer leading to mystical experience of a kind that is not reported in archaic or tribal religion.

Mystical experience of closeness to or even union with the divine is notoriously difficult to put into words, but,

> Although similar to states of feeling, mystical states seem to those who experience them to be also states of knowledge. They are states of insight into depths of truth unplumbed by the discursive intellect. They are illuminations, revelations, full of significance and importance, all inarticulate though they remain; and as a rule they carry with them a curious sense of authority for aftertime.[32]

And,

> In spite of their repudiation of articulate self-description, mystical states in general assert a pretty distinct theoretic drift. It is possible to give the outcome of the majority of them in terms that point in definite philosophical directions. One of these directions is optimism, and the other is monism. We pass into mystical states from out of ordinary consciousness as from a less into a more, as from a smallness into a vastness, and at the same time as from an unrest to a rest. We feel them as reconciling, unifying states.[33]

While many religious believers may not have mystical experience in this sense, prayer could be said to be an absolutely essential aspect of the world religions:

> Religion is an intercourse, a conscious and voluntary relation, entered into by a soul in distress with the mysterious power upon which it feels itself to depend, and upon which its fate is contingent. This intercourse with God is realised by prayer. Prayer is religion in act; that is, prayer is real religion. It is prayer that distinguishes the religious phenomenon from such similar or neighbouring phenomena as purely moral or

aesthetic sentiment. Religion is nothing if it be not the vital act by which the entire mind seeks to save itself by clinging to the principle from which it draws its life.[34]

This growing significance of the inner life of the individual also manifests itself in a new consciousness of the need for self-awareness and 'know thyself' becomes, in one form or another, a general maxim. Intentions and motives are closely scrutinised, and an increasingly sophisticated range of psychological concepts develops. The emphasis on physical purity shifts to purity of mind and heart, and moral courage becomes more important than the merely physical variety while in the realm of law the mental element is increasingly recognised.

For the first time 'religion' therefore emerges as something distinct from society in the modern manner, and this also created the possibility of new forms of social conflict. The great teachers all had to get their message of truth accepted since they did not speak from any prior position of authority, but emerged in an atmosphere of controversy, criticising accepted ideas, and this meant that they had to convince enough of their contemporaries for their ideas to survive. Religion was now a system of explicit beliefs that were held to be true rather than implicit assumptions and ritual practices, and because it developed in reaction to traditional religion we find the development of creeds, sets of doctrines that could bind believers together, regardless of their social identity, and this had very important consequences. Apart from the new possibilities of converting foreign unbelievers, (or fighting them), it also created the possibilities of new loyalties and new divisions within societies and provided a formidable basis for a new type of religious elite to criticise rulers and society in general. The Stoics had developed the idea that a man is a member of two commonwealths. One is the state and the other is humanity at large, with which one's ties are moral or religious rather than legal or political and which might have a higher authority than that of the state, an idea that could easily be developed into the supremacy of the Kingdom of Heaven.

(d) *The moralisation of religion*

The 'moralisation of religion' involved very much more than the idea of God issuing commandments. In the first place the inner life of the morally developed individual required constant self-examination, and in China the idea of introspection (*nei-sheng*, 'to look within') was basic to the attainment of virtue in Confucianism. In the *Analects*, Tseng, the disciple of Confucius, says for example: 'I daily examine myself on three points – In planning for others have I failed in conscientiousness? In intercourse with friends have I been insincere? And have I failed to practise what I have been taught?'(*An*.1.4). For Buddhism:

> True morality is not confined to the external act of the doer but, rather, relates to his mental purity. He has not only to put a curb on ethically wrong actions but also, through conscious effort, to constantly train his mind to deter it from harbouring ethically wrong notions and desires. There should be perfect harmony between his actions and his thoughts, ethically pure actions springing forth from an ethically pure mind.[35]

One of the most obvious and profound changes in moral understanding and in the structure of ethical systems is therefore the much greater significance of the individual and the life of inner moral and spiritual experience. With the breakdown of these stable social systems based upon inherited status, the individual was now forced to become more conscious of himself as an agent who had to choose and decide between a variety of possible courses of action and ways of life, and this was especially true in urban and commercial situations. But this new awareness of the individual and especially of the inner life did not have all the connotations of modern Western individualism, especially with its atomistic associations of egotism and selfishness.

In the first place, the individual was not thought of as having some kind of reality that was prior to, or independent of, society. For all except the Epicureans and other materialists, Man is essentially a social being even if renunciation of society at some period of life is accepted as morally or spiritually valuable. Individualism in the egoistic sense of making one's own interests the chief criterion of action is strongly condemned, and there is no idea of individual rights in the modern Western sense; duties, not rights are what are important. Nor, correspondingly, is there much idea of the importance of uniqueness and the romantic European notion that 'the moral man should express his uniqueness in his life in a manner akin to the original artist in his creative act'[36] is generally absent.

Despite the different emphases on reason, or revelation, or asceticism, as the sources of enlightenment, we find that all the traditions we are considering asserted that *virtue, wisdom, and happiness are inseparably linked,* and that selfishness in general and the passions in particular are the prime source of unhappiness by preventing us attaining the goal of tranquillity of mind. As the Dalai Lama has recently been quoted, when asked what is the meaning of life[37]:

'The meaning of life is happiness.'... 'Hard question is not, "What is meaning of life?" That is easy question to answer. No, hard question is what make happiness. Money? Big house? Accomplishment? Friends? Or...' He paused. 'Compassion and good heart? This question all human beings must try to answer: What make true happiness?'

Wisdom is an essential aspect of this moral growth by which the moral agent comes to understand what is truly right, and so obtains inner tranquillity of mind and true happiness and, in a religious context, salvation. The keys to this end are therefore self-knowledge and self-control. In Buddhism, 'When one has overcome all desires, such inveterate tendencies of mind as attachment, malice, hatred, envy and illusions are automatically annihilated and one comes to possess complete equanimity of mind'.[38]

In the Christian tradition, 'The self that is realised in religion is beyond the conscious ego; it is a wider self, often experienced as a power from beyond the ego, bringing as a gift a quality of life unobtainable by purely self-conscious effort, which both enlarges moral sensitivity and also brings a sense of eternity and mindfulness to the knower'.[39]

The general agreement is therefore that there are certain virtues of special importance for the complete human being; the cultivation of these puts us in the proper relation to cosmos and to society, and will produce a state of harmony or health within us so leading to tranquillity of mind and invulnerability to fortune. Virtue can only be attained by a long process of training and self-scrutiny involving a lifetime of struggle. As the Stoics said, 'The virtue of the happy man and a well-run life consists in this: that all actions are based on the principle of harmony with his own spirit and the will of the Director of the universe'.[40]

This powerful and important doctrine for right living was worked out in great philosophical detail in Greece, India, and China; we do not find it in explicit form in the Old Testament which was not philosophically minded, but in the New Testament St. Paul added the religious virtues of faith, hope, and charity to the classical virtues of justice, reasonableness, courage, and self-control. Muslim philosophers, too, found no difficulty in combining Greek ideas on virtue with the tenets of Islam. 'The two central questions... for most ethical writers in Islam, both philosophical and religious, are the nature and conditions of virtue, on the one hand, and the attainment of happiness on the other'.[41] William James sums up what he calls 'a certain composite photograph of universal saintliness, the same in all religions'. They are:

1. A feeling of being in a wider life than that of this world's selfish little interests; and a conviction, not merely intellectual, but as it were sensible, of the existence of an Ideal Power...

2. A sense of the friendly continuity of the ideal power with our own life, and a willing self-surrender to its control.

3. An immense elation and freedom, as the outlines of the confining selfhood melt down.

4. A shifting of the emotional centre towards loving and harmonious affections, towards "yes, yes", and away from "no", where the claims of the non-ego are concerned.

These fundamental conditions have characteristic consequences, as follows:

Asceticism. The self-surrender may become so passionate as to turn to self-immolation. It may then so overrule the ordinary inhibitions of the flesh that the saint finds positive pleasure in sacrifice and asceticism, measuring and expressing as they do the degree of his loyalty to the higher power.

Strength of Soul. The sense of enlargement of life may be so uplifting that personal motives and inhibitions, commonly omnipotent, become too insignificant for notice, and new reaches of patience and fortitude open out. Fears and anxiety go, and blissful equanimity takes their place...

Purity. The shifting of the emotional centre brings with it, first, increase of purity. The sensitiveness to spiritual discords is enhanced, and the cleansing of existence from brutal and sensual elements becomes imperative. Occasions of contact with such elements are avoided: the saintly life must deepen its spiritual consistency and keep unspotted from the world. In some temperaments this need of purity takes an ascetic turn, and weaknesses of the flesh are treated with relentless severity.

Charity. The shifting of the emotional centre brings, secondly, increase of charity, tenderness for fellow-creatures. The ordinary motives to antipathy, which usually set such close bounds to tenderness among human beings, are inhibited. The saint loves his enemies, and treats loathsome beggars as his brothers.[42]

Virtue is also an essential part of the social order since not only does a society of virtuous people work better than a society of vicious people, but because there are certain key social roles, such as parent and child, subject and ruler and friend, whose proper performance is necessary for the good of the social order and these roles require the appropriate virtues if they are to be performed properly. Aristotle put the balance between individual and society as follows: 'If *all* were to strive towards what is noble and strain every nerve to do the noblest deeds, everything would be as it should be for the common good, and everyone would secure for himself the goods that are greatest, since virtue is the greatest of goods'.

A major development in the content of virtue which we have already noted is the marked growth in the spirit of love, of compassion and benevolence towards one's fellows, which is found in all the cultures of our study. In the New Testament love is made the central principle, as in the commandments to love God with all our hearts and minds and our neighbours as ourselves, upon which hang all the law and the prophets. In China, too, the Confucians made *jen*, human-heartedness, benevolence, or compassion, their central virtue and the Mohists went even further in their demands for universal love. 'The meaning of virtue', says Confucius, 'is "love your fellow men"', and when asked if there is any word which could be adopted as a lifelong rule of conduct replies 'Is not sympathy the word?' While Confucius said little about Heaven, the Mohists believed that '...Heaven loves the whole world universally. Everything is prepared for the good of Man. Even the tip of a hair is the work of Heaven... It sends down snow, frost, rain and dew to grow the five grains, hemp, and silk, thereby enabling people to gain and be benefited by these'.[43]

In Buddhism, love of one's fellows is a central teaching:

As regards the place of love in Buddhism, let us quote a passage from the *Digha Nikaya* which should settle the issue: 'All the means that can be used as bases for right actions are not worth the sixteenth part of the emancipation of the heart through love. This takes all others into itself, outshining them in glory. Just as whatsoever stars there be, their radiance avails not the sixteenth part of the radiance of the moon, just as the sun, mounting up into a clear and cloudless sky, overwhelms all darkness in the realms of space, so all means to right actions avail not the sixteenth part of the emancipation of the heart through love.[44]

In traditional cultures before the Axial Age pride and a keen sense of one's own honour and worth were highly admired. While realistic self-confidence and legitimate pride in work well done are quite proper, pride in the sense of having to feel superior to others, and narcissistic self-absorption came to be regarded as a deadly sin in all the world religions. It sets up the self as the object of worship and cuts us off from God and our neighbour and hence humility received a new emphasis. Humility is often thought of as a distinctive, and eccentric, teaching of Christianity demanding a morbid spirit of grovelling and self-abasement. Because the ego and vanity and self-deception are such powerful human temptations, humility was in fact highly valued as an essential feature of the moral life all across the ancient world, and every religion has emphasised its central importance.

Humility was certainly fundamental to Buddhist ideas of

moral growth: 'It is easy to see the faults of others, but difficult to see one's own faults. 'One shows the faults of others like chaff winnowed in the wind, but one conceals one's own faults as a cunning gambler conceals his dice.' (*Dh.* 252-3) 'Look upon the man who tells thee thy faults as if he told thee of a hidden treasure, the wise man who shows thee the dangers of life' (*Dh.*76). And in the Hindu *Laws of Manu* it was said 'A priest should always be alarmed by adulation as if it were poison and always desire scorn as if it were ambrosia.'[45]

Confucius was remarkable for his humility:

The Master said: 'In literature perhaps I may compare with others, but as to my living the noble life, to that I have not yet attained... As to being a sage or a man of virtue, how dare I presume to such a claim? But as to striving thereafter unwearyingly, and teaching others without flagging, – that can be said of me, and that is all' (*An.*7.32-33). 'When you see a man of worth, think how to rise to his level. When you see an unworthy man, then look within and examine yourself' (*An.*4.17).

Aristotle would not have recognised humility as a virtue but among the later Stoics we find Seneca writing 'It is of virtue, not of myself, that I am speaking, and my quarrel is against all vices, more especially against my own. When I shall be able, I shall live as I ought' (*De Vita Beata* XVIII.1), and Marcus Aurelius said, 'When thy neighbour's errors offend thee, straightway turn to thyself and consider what sin may be laid to thy charge.' (*Thoughts*, X.30). In Islam humility was also considered an essential virtue. By comparison with the power of God the bravest and richest aristocrat was as nothing, and God was compassionate and merciful, the benevolent as well as omnipotent ruler of the universe. 'Thus it comes about that the element of meekness, or humbleness, as the human counterpart of the benevolence of God, is made the very pivotal point of Islamic ethics'.[46]

Since spiritual pride is in some ways the worst of sins in which the ego replaces God as the centre of existence, humility, its necessary antidote, is expressed in confession:

> It is part of the general system of purgation and cleansing which one feels one's self in need of, in order to be in a right relation to one's deity. For him who confesses, shams are over and realities have begun; he has exteriorised his rottenness. If he has not actually got over it, he at least no longer smears it over with a hypocritical show of virtue – he lives at least upon a basis of veracity.[47]

Religion therefore becomes thoroughly permeated with moral values and one's personal virtue and good actions are necessary for happiness and the salvation of one's soul. We find everywhere a major extension of the morality of the 'good' – of benevolence, mercy, and compassion – towards all people, not just to members of one's own society or even culture. Self-criticism and humility are essential virtues, as well as self-control, courage, and especially wisdom; it is these virtues that equip one not only to perform well in one's community as a human being, but also to attain happiness. The ethics of non-retaliation are part of this development: not only is revenge often deprecated but we find several traditions advocating the ideal of benevolence even to one's enemies. There also develops the idea of a common humanity which transcends the boundaries of nation and culture and social distinctions of rank, such as slavery, so that all good men are brothers and the ideal condition of Man would be universal peace.

(e) *The ancient materialist atheists*
But before we leave the ancient world, where modern forms of

religion first emerged, it is worth taking a brief look at some real atheist materialists who denied that the universe was governed by any meaningful plan, or that Man had any special status in it, and that the chance motions and collisions of atoms were responsible for everything. Their views on ethics followed quite logically from these assumptions, and they are the real intellectual ancestors of modern Humanists. The best known were the Epicureans of Greece, (founded by Epicurus of Samos), but the Lokayatas or Carvakas of India also held very similar beliefs, and the Yangists of China, too, were also materialist atheists, although atomic theory did not develop in China.

They agreed on a number of points: the gods are either non-existent or powerless; there is no inherent order in the cosmos, which is produced by accidental combinations of matter, and therefore there is no purpose or meaning in the general scheme of things; primary importance and reality is ascribed to the individual as a physical being, rather than society; the senses, not logic, give the most reliable information about the world and pleasure is the only important aim in life; there is no evidence for the existence of the soul, which either does not exist at all or, like consciousness, is produced from the material elements of the body and does not survive death. All these schools seem to have been quite indifferent to society and the general good, and to have advocated withdrawal and the pursuit of private satisfactions.

It is therefore not surprising that Epicurus considered the rational pursuit of pleasure (as distinct from thoughtless self-indulgence) to be the primary good, and consistently with this view the traditional virtues of justice, temperance, reasonableness, and courage are only valuable because they lead to pleasure, not because they are good for us in themselves as an essential part of being human. Indeed, he thought that we were not inherently social beings and had no natural leanings towards community life: 'There is no such thing as human society; each individual looks out for himself. There is no one who feels affection for another, except for his own benefit'[48], and social co-operation was based on a mutual truce of egotists simply to refrain from injuring each other. Epicurus was famous for his advocacy of friendship and his followers, who had no political ambitions or desire to serve their society, formed associations of friends, but even here no genuine altruism was involved. Friendship is good because of the pleasure which having friends provides for *us*.

The Lokayatas of India held very similar ideas, except that they were even more anti-social than the Epicureans. The Hindu Vedas were said to have been written by buffoons and crafty priests in order to cheat the people. Caste purity was absurd, because of the universal propensity of mankind to fornication; rites for the dead were a waste of time, and 'Sins and virtues have no meaning, they are only the words with which people are scared to behave in a particular manner advantageous to the priests'.[49]

Pleasure is the sole aim of Man and the theory is entirely individualistic; the social structure seems to be regarded as merely conventional, and there is no need to control passion and instinct since they are nature's legacy to men. The materialists proclaim the doctrine of uncontrolled energy, self-assertion and reckless disregard of all authority. It is not fair that one man should rule and another obey since all men are made of the same stuff, and all moral rules are nothing more than human conventions. They were willing, however, to take part in political life if it enabled them to enjoy the pleasures of despotism and tyranny. It is no accident that these ideas should also seem very modern because ancient and modern atheism share the same logical structure which leads inevitably to the same sorts of ethical systems, as we shall see later in the book when we meet the ancient atheists in modern dress.

4. The basic contributions of religion to ethics

In modern times the world religions claim that the universe makes sense, that it is not simply physical matter but also has a transcendent element that in some way includes or connects with consciousness, that Man in particular has a unique place in it, and each person has a special relationship with the Supreme Being whom we call God, even if they are foetuses, imbeciles, or people with Alzheimer's. This status of Man transcends the boundaries of race, gender, nation, culture, and social class and is the basis of our mutual obligation to respect the dignity of our fellow human beings.

Man is inherently a social being and can only flourish and develop the potential of his nature by growing up within society. But the proper balance between the mutual claims of the individual and society can only be maintained by the mediation of the Divine which stands outside and above all social orders. Without God who legitimises the moral demands of the social order on the one hand, but who also sanctifies the dignity of the individual, on the other, there will be inevitable social pressures either to develop unrestricted individualism or unrestricted totalitarianism.

God not only stands above any particular society but is also believed to be in direct contact with each individual and who, Christianity and the other world religions believe, loves them as being each of unique value. God therefore supports the social order *because* it allows individuals to flourish. But while an ordered society is necessary for human flourishing Christianity does not favour any particular type of political organisation, whether monarchy, republic, or liberal democracy, and human social importance has nothing to do with God's judgement of individual worth.

God wishes individual human beings to flourish and be happy but religion recognises that true and lasting happiness does not depend on 'individualism' in the egotistical sense of placing oneself at the centre of existence, on pride and the pursuit of power, and social success, material pleasures and possessions, but *on the pursuit of virtue* which is central to the love of God. This is one of the distinguishing features of religious ethics as opposed to secular systems of ethics, which try to base themselves on some intellectual principle such as social justice, human rights, or utility:

> When we talk about the virtues, we are answering the question, 'What kind of person should I become?' They are the goal towards which we strive, even if we never become fully that kind of person in this life. A distinct advantage of this approach to ethics, therefore, is that one of its fundamental categories is growth. Ethics is concerned, on this reading, with knowing what we should aim to become and setting ourselves in the direction of that goal... Another advantage of this approach over the action-oriented or the obligation and law-based understanding of ethics is that it attends to the whole person and to the whole of a person's life. Remembering that growth is the key concept, this approach acknowledges that every moment and every circumstance can contribute to the growth of virtue or its opposite... I become, in other words, what I do.[50]

The inner life of the spirit is what is truly valuable and self-fulfilling, and is illuminated by the love of God and prayer to Him, and by self-examination and the cultivation of virtue, not just the traditional virtues of justice, prudence, self-control, and courage, but humility, hope, and above all benevolence, the commandment to love our neighbour as ourselves. This is the counterpart of the love of God, and in the love of our neighbour, Christianity (and the other religions) has a special concern for the poor, the needy, the sick, the suffering, and the outcasts who are specially commended to our compassion. Indeed, Jesus says that whenever we have relieved the hungry, the naked, the sick, and the homeless we have done it to Him and compassion for those who suffer is a central message of the Cross itself.

So while the inner spiritual life, virtue and love of God, is one essential pole of religion our relations with those around us in our family and community form the other. This is why Jesus said that there were two great commandments: to love God, and to love our neighbours as ourselves; 'love' not in the sense of 'liking', but of 'benevolence', of wishing others well. Christian life is not one of solitary individuals, but a communal life, of individuals fully engaged with their families, community, and society at large, because it is in this way that we can most effectively rise above the narrow and ultimately self-defeating preoccupation with self. All religions recognise that, far from being the source of happiness, self-absorption in 'the fat relentless ego', as Iris Murdoch put it, is the one way not to achieve it. Just as Alice discovered in the Looking Glass World that she could only reach the hill by walking away from it, so Jesus said, 'Whosoever shall seek to save his life shall lose it; and whosoever shall lose his life shall preserve it'. Free self-sacrifice for the family and the community is one of those hallmarks of the sacred (as even godless Britain recognises in its respect for Remembrance Day).

In maintaining this delicate balance between the individual and society that is one of the special qualities of religious ethical systems, the theme of personality is of the first importance because God is said to be love, of our Heavenly Father for His children and of the children for their Father. The world religions therefore emphasise the subjective, *personal* relation of each individual with the Creator; and Jesus, Muhammad, Buddha, and Confucius, the prophets and saints, are all personal examples of how to live with whom believers can empathise. In particular, religion emphasises the essential links between 'the ethics of amity' and the family as the human face of ethics: the fatherhood of God and the brotherhood of man. And it is our personal relation with God that allows us to repent and ask forgiveness and to express our gratitude to God for the inestimable gift of life.

It is these personal, family-type relations which are eroded or destroyed by political power structures, markets, and bureaucratic organisation, and the various forces that variously degrade us into machines, animals, or commodities. The centrality of personality is a principle of the very first importance because this humanity is what is necessarily lacking in utopian rationalist schemes, which are essentially about efficiency, pleasure, or various legalistic forms of social order (notably individual rights, liberty, equality and social justice). It is this humanising quality of Christianity which can be also be said to have been lacking in Stoicism, for example. Religion therefore places the emphasis on duties rather than rights, which in the modern world only too easily become excuses for self-assertion, envy, and the exploitation of the community against the common good. The Christian notions of duty, of loving one's neighbour, and of the inherent worth of every individual can accomplish everything that 'human rights' can without all their negative aspects.

Equality is a fundamental concept of morality because we recognise that all human beings, whatever their particular social identity, have some claim on our moral concern, and equality is therefore a central notion of justice and of doing to others as we would like them to do to us. But there is no reason why this moral equality should be translated directly into some form of *social* equality. Indeed, an obsession with social equality can easily become perverted into the legitimation of envy and the politics of grievance. Complex societies inevitably produce hierarchies and inequalities, and in the working of social institutions at every level there are relevant differences between individuals in aptitude, experience, intelligence, and other qualities that justify inequalities, which will vary according to the particular circumstances of the society. Here the religious idea of vocation, of being called to some particular way of life, to some task, however humble it may be, is important:

> God has created me to do Him some definite service, He has committed some work to me, which he has not committed to another, I have my mission. I may never know it in this life, but I shall be told it in the next. I have a part in a great work; I am a link in a chain, a bond of connection between persons. He has not created me for naught. I shall do good. I shall do his work.[51]

Traditional hierarchical social orders based primarily on birth can obviously encourage arrogance and servility (as can modern bureaucracies) but showing respect to those of higher social rank than ourselves is not obviously demeaning or demoralising in itself, especially when the reciprocal obligations between those of different ranks are observed. Egalitarian societies may also work well in some circumstances, but the morally dark side of this type of social order is envy and hatred of excellence, and the desire to level down all distinction and achievement to the lowest common denominator. All in all, therefore, there seems to be no principled reason for regarding either hierarchical or egalitarian societies as innately superior to the other – it all depends on the moral spirit in which they are operated. Religion accepts the inevitability of differences in social rank and status but regards these as essentially superficial by comparison with real personal worth.

Liberty is also a central religious value, because God is believed to have given us free will to choose or to reject Him, and there is no point in having free will if we cannot exercise it. But no religion advocates liberty for its own sake: it must obviously be exercised responsibly and morally, and it was in this spirit that St Augustine said 'Love God and do what you will, for the soul trained in love to God will do nothing to offend the One who is Beloved', and in a similar way the Book of Common Prayer says of God that 'His service is perfect freedom'. It is clear that there are pathological extremes both of personal autonomy and of social restraint. A society in which there was unlimited personal freedom would be one in which freedom itself was not worth having. On the other hand, tyrannical social orders, especially modern totalitarian regimes, are morally disastrous because they reduce individuals to a kind of child-like status of conformity through fear. The opportunity freely to participate in the working of one's own social institutions is therefore part of what is involved in maturing as a moral agent, but this does not imply that all must or could have an *equal* say in the process.

Finally, it is true that the notion of God as law-giver has been the basis of a primitive self-interested legalism in which the individual is only motivated by hope of reward in Heaven and fear of punishment in Hell. No doubt this has been extremely useful for maintaining law and order and is to this extent very much better than nothing, but if we thought our neighbour was only restrained from robbing our house or murdering us by his fear of damnation, we would think him a pretty poor moral specimen. It is possible, however, to use the relation of God to Man as the basis for an entirely different motivation for moral conduct: the imitation of an admired example out of love. In the same way, the true craftsman aims for perfection in his work because he loves it for its own sake, not because he hopes to sell it for more money. So Aquinas contrasts the Old Law (of Israel) with the New Law (of Christ): '...it belongs to law to induce men to observe its commandments. This the Old Law did by the fear of punishment, but the New Law, by love, which is poured into our hearts by the grace of Christ, bestowed in the New Law, but foreshadowed in the Old' (*Summa Theologica* II.91.6). And as the Sufi woman Saint Rabi'a expressed it: 'God, if I worship Thee in fear of hell, burn me in hell. And if I worship Thee in hope of Paradise, exclude me from Paradise; but if I worship Thee for

Thine own sake, withhold not Thine everlasting Beauty'.[52] Similarly, if the essence of Heaven is closeness to God, then damnation is our own self-exclusion from the presence of God by our own wickedness. As William Law said, 'Men are not in hell because God is angry with them; they are in wrath and darkness because they have done to the light, which infinitely flows forth from God, as that man does to the light of the sun, who puts out his own eyes'.[53]

To sum up, then, religious ethics absorbs secular ethics about good social conduct and good citizenship as something believers and non-believers should adhere to as a matter of course. It is in the higher aspects of ethics, the ideals rather than the basic social duties, that religious ethics makes its distinctive contribution and it has at least the following aspects: it gives us a special place in the universe and is the only basis for the moral unity of the human race; it emphasises the importance of individual human dignity and includes here physical as well as moral dignity; it maintains the delicate moral balance between the dignity of the individual and the requirements of the social order and God provides an alternative to the worship of either the Self or the State; it is very much an ethic of virtue, rather than of rules and rights in the modern secular fashion; it celebrates humility and rejects pride, egocentrism, and the worship of the Self as utterly opposed to right living; it places the spiritual above the material and rejects the worship of material success, physical pleasures, and mere worldly values; it contrasts the fleeting vanities of this world with the eternal values of goodness and truth; and therefore it turns our social priorities of success and power upside down, with a special concern for the poor, weak, and outcast rather than for the rich and important.

One final point is this. In the first chapter we saw how certain features of human nature make it easy for us to behave as co-operative, sympathetic, and sociable human beings, but the ethical ideals of the world religions in important ways go against the grain of human nature by their austere demands. In particular, self-denial, humility, and the path of virtue are all hard roads to travel, and the whole religious tradition is that we have to wrestle, in certain respects, with some of our basic human impulses and bodily desires to attain salvation. Human nature may therefore have set us off in some basic respects as capable of attaining the good, but by itself human nature is not enough and can be a positive hindrance. The difficulty of living up to the Sermon on the Mount is a case in point.

It will be clear to anyone who reads the newspapers that the picture I have been giving of religious ethics is very much an ideal that is often violated, sometimes grossly, in everyday life by some of those who profess to be religious believers. Fundamentalist Muslims are obvious examples at the present time, but in past centuries much the same accusations could have been levelled against Catholics and Protestants.

Organised religion has been no exception to that general opposition between the ethics of amity and enmity which we discussed in the first chapter, and just as human beings have fought over race, nationality, class, language and political ideology, organised religion from early times has been no exception to the general rule that what unites some people will also divide them from others. Religion also became closely involved in providing legitimacy for rulers and this involvement with worldly authority and social prestige, and with nationalism, inevitably had a corrupting influence. In our personal lives, too, there is also the general question of why religious people have notoriously been capable of so much evil. In answer to this, William Law said:

They have turned to God without turning from themselves; would be alive to God before they are dead to their own nature. Now religion in the hands of self, or corrupt nature, serves only to discover vices of a worse kind than in nature left to itself. Hence are all the disorderly passions of religious men, which burn in a worse flame than passions only employed about worldly matters. Pride, self-exaltation, hatred and persecution, under a cloak of religious zeal, will sanctify actions which nature, left to itself, would be ashamed to own.[54]

Chapter 3

Humanism

1. Science and religion

Throughout recorded history there have been non-religious people who have believed that this life is the only life we have, that the universe is a natural phenomenon with no supernatural side, and that we can live ethical and fulfilling lives on the basis of reason and humanity. They have trusted to the scientific method, evidence, and reason to discover truths about the universe and have placed human welfare and happiness at the centre of their ethical decision making. (From the *British Humanist Association* website)

Far from having been around 'throughout recorded history', the scientific method only developed with Galileo and his contemporaries; the ideas of the ancient atomists were forgotten for many centuries until revived by seventeenth-century chemists, and the general idea that 'religion' and 'science' have always been locked in conflict is simplistic and unhistorical. Religious thought has many strands; some of these have clearly been hostile to the scientific study of nature, but others have been much more favourable and we must also distinguish the personal faith of individuals from 'religion' in the form of official Churches, or equivalent bodies.

Religious explanations of nature are most obviously irrational and anti-scientific when they simply appeal to the will of a deity. For example, 'Why does water expand when it freezes?' 'Because that is God's will.' No sense can be made of statements like this, which simply 'explain' one unknown by another. Religious traditions that emphasise the omnipotence of God at the expense of

His rationality are clearly liable to fall into this category.

Some Indian thinkers, especially the Buddhists, thought that the picture of the physical world given by our senses is an illusion, *maya*, so that studying it could only be a waste of time. This profound devaluation of the whole of material existence, by comparison with the spiritual, could produce in any religion what Joseph Needham has called a 'holy ignorance' that stifled all intellectual enquiry into nature. Some took the view that even if the physical world is not an illusion, by comparison with eternity it is trivial and not worth serious attention. A more hostile view of the study of nature was that trying to understand its mysteries was not just idle curiosity that led to the sin of pride, but positively impious: 'To pry into the mysteries of nature that God chose not to reveal... was to transgress the boundary of legitimate intellectual inquiry, to challenge God's majesty, and to enter into the territory of forbidden knowledge.'[1]

Even if there was religious interest in nature, as in the early Middle Ages, this might only consist in finding symbolic references to the divine. For example,

> The pelican, which was believed to nourish its young with its own blood, was the analogue of Christ who feeds mankind with his own blood. In such a world there was no thought of hiding behind a clump of reeds actually to observe the habits of a pelican. There would have been no point in it. Once one had grasped the spiritual meaning of the pelican, one lost interest in individual pelicans.[2]

There has also been a tendency for religious leaders to regard secular explanations of the natural world as a challenge to their own intellectual authority. This raises the distinction between religion as the personal faith of individual believers, and religion as a social institution. Until well into the nineteenth century European scientists themselves were mostly believing Christians who saw nothing incompatible between science and religion; indeed, they regarded the Book of Nature as well as the Bible as God's handiwork. The struggles that occurred were not so much between science and *religion* as between scientists and the authority of the Church.

On the other hand, there were a number of reasons why religion could foster serious scientific enquiry. In the first place the study of the heavenly bodies and the calendar was an integral aspect of religion from very early times, and this astrology laid the essential foundations of Greek astronomy, the first of the exact sciences. More generally, ancient religions were very interested in how the cosmos was formed by the gods. How things began, the emergence of the first humans, and so on, are standard themes in the myths of tribal societies and the ancient literate civilisations. These creation myths were therefore important sources from which the earliest rational speculation about the nature of things could develop, as we can see in the Pre-Socratic philosophers.

But undoubtedly the most important stimulus here came from those notions discussed in the previous chapter, of Logos, Bráhman, or Tao, with the whole idea that the universe makes sense at some deep level, and that it is governed by a unified body of rational laws given by a Supreme Being. This has been an essential belief for the development of natural science, and unless the Greeks, in particular, had been convinced of this they would never have persevered in the serious investigations of nature that they did, and the same is true of medieval and Renaissance science. It was through St Augustine in particular that the ideas of 'laws of nature', that could be applied to the workings of the heavenly bodies, and to natural processes on earth, passed into Western thought, and provided the idea that the mind of God could be discovered in the book of nature as well as in the scriptures.[3]

Copernicus, Kepler, and Newton, for example, were firmly in

this tradition. As Joseph Needham says, '...historically the question remains whether natural science could ever have reached its present stage of development without passing through a "theological stage"'[4], that is, of a rational Creator giving laws to the natural world as well as to Man, and which Man could understand. The ancient idea that the scientific study of the natural world is to study the mind of God remained an extremely important motivation for genuinely scientific studies until well into the nineteenth century, and still survives.[5]

But given the importance that Humanists ascribe to science, and the revolutionary claims of modern biology about the nature of Man, it is quite striking that the only interest they seem to have in biology is using it to attack religion, not to reflect on what it has to say about Man. Yet if one takes the claims of evolutionary biologists seriously, especially their denial of consciousness and free will, it is hard to see how the very idea of human agency and moral responsibility could survive at all. Although Humanists prefer to ignore these issues, in the words of Francis Crick, 'tomorrow's science is going to knock their culture right out from under them'[6], and they need to come to terms with the obvious incompatibility between their liberal Western values and a genuinely Darwinian view of Man.

2. The Humanist tradition

Contrary to the claims of the Humanist Association website, contemporary atheistic Humanism is really a modern phenomenon dating from the nineteenth century. The first 'Humanists' were fourteenth-century Italians rediscovering the literature of classical Greece and Rome. This *'literae humanae'*, 'human literature', opened up a much wider range of knowledge and human creativity than the earlier 'divine literature' of the Scriptures and the Church Fathers, even though Aquinas in particular had reconciled much of Aristotle with Christian doctrine. But while the Humanists were in revolt against the medieval scholasticism of the Roman Church, and some criticised various aspects of its teachings and practices, their attitude to religion covered a wide range: Erasmus, Thomas More, and Tyndale were as much men of the Renaissance as sceptics like Machiavelli and Montaigne and, indeed, the Humanist emphasis on the importance of Greek for understanding the New Testament was a powerful influence behind the Reformation itself. Many pagan works, especially by Plato and Cicero, were also regarded as generally consistent with Christian beliefs rather than as being a danger to them: 'Moralists believed that from Classical poets, philosophers, moralists, historians, and statesmen – above all from Xenophon, Seneca, Cicero, and Livy – models of virtue could be derived which the truly civilized man could pursue, in harmony with the Christian's progress towards spirituality and salvation'.[7] Indeed, Cicero's *De Officiis*, 'On Duty', was a standard textbook on ethics for English schoolboys until well into the nineteenth century, who knew it as 'Tully's Offices'.

The later Renaissance saw the beginning of modern science, with such figures as Galileo, Kepler, and Newton, and that general development of scientific and rationalistic thought in the late seventeenth and eighteenth centuries known as 'The Enlightenment'. It placed the greatest value on Reason as the essential basis of human progress, especially as demonstrated in the natural sciences but although thoroughly sceptical of the historical truth of the Bible, and extremely hostile to the Roman Catholic Church in particular because of its history of perse-cution, intolerance, and suppression of intellectual freedom, Enlightenment thinkers were not, at least for the most part, actually *atheistic* and still accepted the idea of a Supreme Being. 'Advanced thinkers tended not so much to be hostile to Christianity per se, or to religion in general, but were rather concerned to achieve a purified, refined expression of faith, which would be commensurable with reason and science, conscience and probability. Countless educated people could see no reason why such a faith ('true religion') should be an obstacle to progress.'[8]

Until well into the nineteenth century science could co-exist with religion, if not so easily with the Catholic Church, because both could subscribe to the belief in a rationally ordered universe which made sense, but the growing idea that the universe and life might be meaningless accidents was completely incompatible with religion. G.M.Young said, 'If I were asked what the total effect of Darwin, Mill, Huxley, and Herbert Spencer upon their age had been, I should answer somehow thus. They made it difficult, almost to impossibility, for their younger contemporaries to retain the notion of a transcendent, governing Providence'.[9] The world-views of Thomas Hardy and A.E.Housman are good examples of this pervasive sense of despair, considering human life as nothing more than, in Housman's words, 'a long fool's errand to the grave'. While modern Humanists, therefore, like to borrow the clothes of their Renaissance predecessors, or even those of the Greeks, they are essentially a nineteenth-century phenomenon.

Dawkins, Hitchens, and most contemporary atheists advocate the moral values of Humanism, but to give some focus and coherence to this critique of modern Humanism, I shall concentrate mainly on the work of two well-known philosophers, Professor A.C.Grayling's *The God Argument: the Case against Religion and for Humanism* (2013), and Professor Paul Kurtz's *Forbidden Fruit: the Ethics of Secularism* (2008), which it is fair to treat as authoritative accounts of twenty-first-century Humanism. According to Grayling, Humanism has 'Two basic premises: that there are no supernatural agencies in the universe, and that ethics must be based on our experience.' (147). But he denies that Humanism is any kind of philosophy or system of thought: 'When people submit to systems, they are handing over to them (to those who devised them) the right to do their

105

thinking and choosing for them'(152). 'Standardly, a philosophy is a fully fleshed-out affair... a metaphysics... But humanism requires no commitment to teachings beyond its two fundamental premises, and it imposes no obligations on people other than to think for themselves' (149).

The ideal Humanist is presented to us with remarkable clarity: his basic personal duty is to himself, and rather than developing his virtue he is encouraged to develop his talents; the personal qualities that are given the most emphasis are being the master of one's own destiny and the ability to enjoy life. Humanists regard autonomy as crucial: 'Among the highest human excellences is a person's ability to take control of his or her own life' (Kurtz, 150), and the other major emphasis is on success and enjoying life – 'eating the fruit of the tree of life', in Paul Kurtz's phrase. But being the master of one's own destiny would be meaningless without free will, something denied by materialists, so it is interesting that while, as I have said, Humanists are immensely enthusiastic about science and materialism in general when they are attacking religion, they dodge the whole question of free will in a few lines (Kurtz, 79-80: Grayling, 171), and simply assert its existence, while the problems about the material basis of consciousness, and its implications, are not mentioned at all. Here, as elsewhere, they fall back on the traditions of Christian civilisation when in difficulty.

In a list of those qualities that make up personal excellence, Kurtz places autonomy first of all, as I have said, then intelligence, self-discipline, self-respect, creativity, motivation, affirmation, health, joie-de-vivre, and aesthetic appreciation, and some typical fruits from the humanist tree of life are climbing mountains, listening to symphonies or reading sonnets, and enjoying sex or a fine banquet, or the elegance of a mathematical proof. For Grayling, the humanist ideal is very similar: 'the humanist is one who seeks to be informed, reflective, alert, responsive, eager for understanding and for achievement of the good: in short, to be a good guest at the dinner of life' (140).

We are also given a detailed programme of what all right-thinking people should believe about human rights, sexual morality, abortion, euthanasia, parenting, education, privacy, crime and punishment, vegetarianism, animal rights, separation of church and state, and government. This seems a remarkably detailed set of conclusions to draw from the two simple premises of 'no supernatural beings', and 'thinking for oneself', but in fact none of it follows from these at all. What we are actually getting here is a highly ethnocentric summary of the fashionable opinions of Western secular liberals in the early twenty-first century, and who in Britain would read the *Guardian*. Indeed, not just modern Western liberals, but well-educated and comfortably-off liberals of the sort who would know what to talk about and what to wear as 'good guests at the dinner of life' at an Oxford or Cambridge High Table.

3. The glorification of success

Clearly, then, Humanism is a prolonged glorification of Self, success, and the gratification in every possible way of 'the fat, relentless ego', which is why it has a particular loathing of religion:

> The meaning of life is not to be found in a secret formula discovered by ancient prophets or priests, who withdraw from it in quiet contemplation and release. It can be discovered by anyone and everyone who can untap an inborn zest for living. It is found within living itself, as it reaches out to create new conditions of experience. Eating of the fruit of the tree of life gives us the bountiful enthusiasm for living. The 'ultimate' value for the humanist is the conviction that life can be found good in and of itself. Each moment has a kind of preciousness and attractiveness... Perhaps it is because the dour and fearful religionist concentrates all 'meaning' on God

and on his hope for a future life that he cannot fully enjoy these experiences, and hence, in a vicious circle, has to look outside his own life for meaning (Kurtz, 297).

It is also very much a matter for the intellectual and social elite who can pick the most luscious fruit from 'the tree of life', with not much left for ordinary people, let alone the poor and the outcast. For example, 'Perhaps the most basic personal duty a person has is *to be all that he is capable of being, to utilize his talents, and to realize his capacities.* Capacities, of course, are multifarious, and generally cannot all be realized. Should one become a mathematician or a violinist, a great lover or a chef, an athlete or a businessman, a peace activist or a scientist?' (Kurtz, 173)

This is a remarkably elitist set of occupations, more appropriate to Hollywood and to '*Lifestyles of the Rich and Famous*' than to ordinary life, where the options for the majority are likely to be rather less exciting, like working in a factory or an office, or being unemployed. Again, the Humanist enthusiasm for autonomy, and being the master of one's own destiny, is not a luxury that is normally available for the poor. Creativity is particularly important here: 'The creative person exemplifies the most eloquent expression of human freedom: the capacity for originality. Creativity is intimately related to autonomy and self-respect, for the independent person has some sense of his own power.' (Kurtz, 156) And it is not hard to see that Grayling's 'good guests at the dinner of life', with a keen sense of their own power, are going to be the rich, talented, and successful, the high-powered business executives and bankers, politicians, media stars, doctors, lawyers, and academics, especially in North America and Europe.

Absorbed as they are in consuming the fruits of the tree of life, the Humanists therefore seem to have no thought for those millions of destitute and suffering for whom they are out of reach, and for the illiterate masses who would make poor guests indeed at the dinner of life. These people, not just in the developing world, but in all our major cities have no choice but to lead what are often rather pointless and boring lives doing what other people tell them, or unemployed, or in fear of violence, or old and lonely, or sick without the money to pay for medicines, or as subsistence peasants in Africa or Asia or South America. It was to these people that all the great religious leaders spoke, rather than to the wealthy elite, but to whom secular humanists have nothing relevant to say at all. If what really matters is developing one's own talents and potential, how could they have any message for those without the means of doing so?

The humanist emphasis on achievement and success ties in closely to the modern American dogma that one has to love oneself before one can love others, 'Because you're worth it', as the advertising slogan puts it, and to the idea that everyone should think of themselves as special and develop high self-esteem. The self-esteem movement began in the United States in the 1970s, because it was believed that high self-esteem was the answer to the majority of psychological and social problems. 'I cannot think of a single psychological problem – from anxiety and depression, to fear of intimacy or of success, to spouse battering or of child molestation – that is not traceable to the problem of low self-esteem'[10], and '...many, if not most, of the major problems plaguing society have roots in the low self-esteem of many of the people who make up society'.[11] By the late 1980s there was even a National Association for Self-Esteem. In fact, as we might have suspected, low-self esteem does not appear to be a problem for Americans: 'The fact that most people score toward the high end of self-esteem measures casts serious doubt on the notion that American society is suffering from widespread low self-esteem. If anything, self-esteem in America is high'.[12]

It is important to clarify here what we mean by the notion of self-esteem that is being used. On the one hand, high self-esteem 'may refer to an accurate, justified, balanced appreciation of one's worth as a person and one's successes and competencies', but we are all familiar with another kind of self-esteem which involves 'an inflated, arrogant, grandiose, unwarranted sense of conceited superiority over others'. We may call this pathological, just as there can be a pathological sense of insecurity and inferiority which is quite distinct from true humility.[13] The distinction between these two kinds of self-esteem becomes clear when objective measures are applied to performance. For example, 'People with high self-esteem [in the pathological sense] are gorgeous in their own eyes, but objective observers do not see any difference'.[14] While there is a correlation between rational self-esteem and school performance, this self-esteem is a result rather than a cause: 'The evidence does not support the belief that high self-esteem leads to good school performance. Instead, high self-esteem is the result of good school performance, above average IQ, and social background'.[15] The conclusion of a number of studies was that 'accurate self-knowledge would be more useful than high self-esteem' in raising performance in all these areas'. Or, as that well-known philosopher Clint Eastwood remarked, 'A man's got to know his limitations'. 'These findings are at odds with the oftentimes dramatic portrayal of self-esteem as a prime motivating force in human behaviour and of low self-esteem as a key component of human maladjustment'.[16] Given that there is an important delusional quality in self-esteem, and in the whole philosophy of loving oneself, not surprisingly it has been found that 'In normal populations, scores on the Narcissistic Personality Inventory... correlate substantially with self-esteem'[17], but there will be more on this in the next chapter.

So if people who are already living in a society of enormous physical plenty are encouraged to love and admire themselves and generally put themselves first, to think in terms of their rights and entitlements as opposed to their duties, especially the right to be rich, famous and successful, with easy credit and the encouragement to get whatever they want now, with every opportunity for self-advertisement on the social media, and enjoying forms of entertainment dominated by sex and violence, then it is hardly surprising that it will be one long holiday for pride, greed, envy, anger, lust, gluttony, and sloth.

4. Rationalism

Humanism, unlike religion, is said to be defined by its respect for reason: 'Humanism is a philosophical outlook... deliberately so because a key requirement of it is that individuals should think for themselves about what they are and how they should live' (Grayling, 149). Grayling holds the view (completely contradicted by the history of civilisation) that philosophy and religion are totally different, because the essence of religious belief is that it is utterly unthinking and credulous (16-17), in contrast to '...the one humanist obligation: to think' (150); the 'rich ethical outlook' of Humanism is 'all the richer indeed for being the result of reflection as opposed to conditioning or tradition' (255).

> The message is clarion clear: to think for oneself is essential to the good life because what flows from doing so is one's own. If others do the thinking for one, or if orthodoxies or traditions do it, one's life is not one's own. The good and well-lived life is not a servitude, but a service to one's chosen values. So the train of thought goes: freedom is what makes it possible to create meaning in one's life, and the creation of meaning in one's life is the good life itself (172).

The worship of Self here could hardly be more extreme. But Grayling's belief that it is possible for individuals to work out entirely by themselves, in some strange kind of cultural vacuum, the fundamental values and principles of how they should live, or of anything else, for that matter, has rightly been called '...the fatally flawed assumption of many Enlightenment thinkers, namely, that autonomous individuals can freely choose, or will, their moral life'.[18] Learning the intellectual traditions of one's own culture, or of any subject, and the development of critical judgement are not mutually contradictory at all, of course, but mutually necessary.

When we come to the unscientific problems of how we should live, reasoning alone, even when performed by professional philosophers often does not inspire much confidence either. Aristotle is the anthropologist's moral philosopher because he locates the individual squarely within society as a 'social animal'. But when I was an undergraduate and first encountered the ethical theories of modern philosophers such as Hume, Kant, Bentham, Moore, and Ayer, let alone Nietzsche, Sartre and the existentialists, I was struck by two things in particular: the first was that, unlike natural scientists, they all fundamentally disagreed with each other, and secondly, far from providing great insights to ordinary mortals their theories often seemed rather ridiculous. In the words of Omar Khayyam: 'Myself when young did eagerly frequent/Doctor and Saint, and heard great argument/ About it and about: but evermore /Came out by the same door wherein I went'.

Reason is only as good as its assumptions about how the world is, and always seems tempted to oversimplify these. 'The seventeenth century had the wisdom to introduce reason as a useful and even necessary tool for handling human affairs. The Enlightenment and the nineteenth century had the folly to consider it to be not merely necessary but even sufficient for the solution of all problems'.[19] A classic example from the Enlightenment is Bentham's ethical theory of Utilitarianism which assumed that the basic human motives are simply to seek pleasure, as the only good, and avoid pain, as the only evil. It therefore followed mathematically that, since 'each is to count for one, and no more than one', 'the greatest happiness of the greatest number is the measure of right and wrong'.

While Utility is a perfectly sensible test of a piece of government legislation, (such as the extension of licensing hours to see if this reduces public drunkenness), as *the* moral principle of private conduct it is strikingly inadequate. Of course we should try to benefit others and not do them harm, but that is only one test among many that distinguishes right from wrong and good from evil. It ignores all principles of justice and fairness, all reference to virtue and kindness, all the requirements of the social and moral order, and, in particular, our *experience* of our relations with family, friends, neighbours, and the wider society. Our daily lives are taken up with performing duties that are inescapable parts of our jobs, or our roles as 'father' or 'neighbour', or 'friend', or 'employee', not actions which we choose specifically because of their pleasure-to-pain ratio. Indeed, once we start thinking of good actions as those which are fitting or appropriate, or in an organic fashion as contributing to the functioning of some kind of larger social whole, in relation to a variety of moral principles, the very notion of treating 'rightness' as something that could be calculated from a kind of pointer reading on a utility-scale, like the boiler pressure of some Victorian steam engine, seems completely misplaced and incongruous. Now we know that Bentham suffered from Asperger's Syndrome[20] we can see why he developed such a morally stunted vision of human life, but it is an interesting reflection on Western society that it should have taken Utilitarianism so very seriously.

So if reason alone is not enough, does this mean that all is hopeless, and that we are condemned to wander in a moral wilderness? If we all had to make up the basic rules of life for ourselves, starting from scratch and without any assistance from others, then we would be, but fortunately we can draw on the accumulated wisdom of the past, and on tradition. What we actually need is to be *reasonable*, rather than rationalistic. We have inherited a vast amount of knowledge and practices from our forebears, much of which are the result of trial and error, and we have to live our lives in the real world, so that to question everything would leave us no time to do anything else at all. Most people are not much good at abstract thought anyway, and live according to a mixture of custom and fashion, in relation to their own *experience* of life. Why would it be absurd for someone to say, 'I'm not particularly clever, and I don't really understand all this philosophical stuff. The way my parents brought me up seems sensible and decent enough for me, and that's how I'm going to try to live my life'? Anyone who has seen the changes in social attitudes and moral values since the 1960s, for example, will find it hard to accept that these are the outcomes of millions of rational individuals, each independently and critically surveying the statistical evidence, and pondering the ethical implications of every issue such as human rights, homosexuality, and abortion, rather than being, overwhelmingly, the result of cultural fashions and social pressures, in forming which the ideas and influence of a small minority of opinion-makers and legis-lators have been disproportionately great.

Custom and taboo can actually play an essential part in preserving the decencies of life, both in private and public life. Constitutional monarchy in Britain and in other countries, for example, is an excellent example of an archaic institution that, far from being based on 'reason' is surrounded by custom and taboo, but has nevertheless been an extremely effective pillar of the social order. Looking back on the liberal rationalist theory of his youth at Cambridge in the circle of Moore, Russell, and Lytton Strachey, John Maynard Keynes concluded that:

> ...it was flimsily based, as I now think, on an *a priori* view of what human nature is like, both other peoples and our own, which was disastrously mistaken (1949:98), ...It was a Utopian view, according to which the human race... consists of reliable, rational, decent people, influenced by truth and objective

standards, who can be safely released from the outward restraints of convention and traditional standards and inflexible rules of conduct, and left, from now onwards, to their own sensible devices, pure motives and reliable intuitions of the good... We were not aware that civilisation was a thin and precarious crust erected by the personality and will of a very few, and only maintained by rules and conventions skilfully put across and guilefully preserved. We had no respect for traditional wisdom or the restraints of custom... It did not occur to us to respect the extraordinary accomplishment of our predecessors in the ordering of life (as it now seems to me to have been) or the elaborate framework which they had devised to protect this order (99-100).

The great moral traditions of antiquity and the world religions, unlike the Babel of modern thought, actually form a remarkable consensus on the basic principles of how we should live despite their other theological differences.

5. The Humanist critique of religion

The underlying theme of modern Humanism is that God is a miserable tyrant, and that to exalt human beings at His expense is a form of liberation from an ogre, rather as the American Colonists liberated themselves from King George III in the War of Independence. Humanists, as atheists, therefore not only consider religion false, but also wish to eradicate it because they think it is harmful. It would, however, be quite consistent for atheists to consider religion as false but *useful* (quite a number do), and an obvious defence of religion is the comfort and consolation it brings to believers, and its strengthening of social bonds.

Numerous modern studies show that the mental and physical health and well-being among active members of churches or similar types of group are significantly greater than among non-believers, and there are good physiological and psychological reasons why this should be so. We now know that there are close links between the brain and the neuro-endocrine system (producing hormones), the immune system, and the cardio-vascular system, so that beliefs, emotions, and some aspects of social life have distinct health implications over a wide range of medical conditions. Very large numbers of surveys have established that stress, depression, a feeling that life is pointless, anger and hostility, loneliness and isolation, and a sense of hopelessness and impotence all have distinctly negative consequences for physical as well as mental well-being. If we think of religion as comprising beliefs about the meaning of life and the presence of God, practices such as private prayer and meditation, and social relationships like attending church with a social support group it becomes clear why we could expect it to be beneficial to the health of believers.

Of the mechanisms proposed to explain the links between religion and health, especially mental health, the factor that provides about 20-30 per cent of the link between religious involvement and health is what has been called the Coherence and Meaning hypothesis: '...religion benefits health by providing a sense of coherence and meaning so that people understand their role in the universe, the purpose of life, and develop the courage to endure suffering'.[21] Spiritual beliefs are therefore major sources of personal strength, and here it is the sincerity of faith, not mere conventionality, or what is often called 'intrinsic' as opposed to 'extrinsic' religion that is most important. Believers report more meaning in life because one is living for one's Maker, not merely for oneself, while belief in a power greater than one's own leads to more self-control. The communal life of religion also plays an essential part in happiness and well-being: for example, in one of the earliest studies of religion and health, Durkheim (1897) showed that active participation in organised religious life was a major factor in preventing suicide (and see Dervic et al. 2004). Attendance at religious services is very strongly related to longevity; rituals have strong positive psychological effects, and prayer is exceptionally powerful. Images of the brain in prayer are like someone interacting with a person they love. Religion also provides the support of close social bonds, larger social networks, more assistance from others, and the satisfaction that comes from this has a marked effect on health.

It is not surprising, therefore, that religious believers score significantly higher in the ability to delay gratification and display self-control, are more forgiving and less revengeful, give more to charity, and have more gratitude for the good things of life – the regular practice of gratitude is apparently a very significant factor in happiness. They also live longer than the norm; have more satisfying marriages; are good at handling physical pain, have better cancer survival rates, and better recovery rates from heart surgery and physical illness generally.[22]

Quite apart from the benefits of sincere religious belief to individual well-being, the value of religion as an agent of social cohesion has long been obvious. It has been an essential feature of political legitimacy from tribal chiefs to kings and emperors, and a potent factor in promoting community solidarity, which is why, of course, religion has always been a central feature of traditional societies. Internationally, the world religions have bound together billions of individuals from every nation and ethnic group.

So if a religious view of the world (at least in the sense of a world that has meaning and purpose, with associated rituals and communal practices) is culturally universal, and seems to provide very significant psychological and physical benefits to believers, should not the Darwinist conclude that religion may have been selected because it strengthens group solidarity, and has been of adaptive value to individuals as a coping mechanism? This is in fact a commonplace view among biologists to explain its universality. As the leading socio-biologist E.O.Wilson says, echoing what we saw in Chapter 1 about group altruism,

If success of the group requires spartan virtues and self-denying religiosity, victory can more than recompense the surviving faithful in land, power, and the opportunity to reproduce. The average individual will win this Darwinian game, and his gamble will be profitable, because the summed efforts of the participants give the average member a more than compensatory advantage (Wilson 2004:187).

Individually, too,

In the midst of the chaotic and potentially disorienting experiences each person undergoes daily, religion classifies him, provides him with unquestioned membership in a group claiming great powers, and by this means gives him a driving purpose in life compatible with his self-interest. His strength is the strength of the group, his guide the sacred covenant (188).

Dawkins and other atheists reply, however, that religion is a pathological evolutionary development, a harmful meme or virus of the mind, and focus exclusively on its negative aspects. The version of religion presented by the Humanists is not based on a dispassionate survey of the evidence but is an extreme caricature of biblical puritanical fundamentalism, of an exceptionally rigid and joyless type, and opposed to all forms of pleasure and scientific knowledge, credulous and totally subject to what are claimed to be the unalterable commands of an inscrutable God. Humanists also like to present Christians in particular as thoroughly ineffectual, paralysed by morbid fear, self-doubt and fatalistic resignation: 'Theists demean human power when they maintain that we are nothing in ourselves but are dependent upon God at every turn. They insist that we can do nothing outside of God's dictates.' (Kurtz, 150) They 'wish to repeal the modern world and return humankind to an earlier age of dependence and obedience to theological authority. They lack confidence in the ability of humans to use reason and science to solve their problems' (11). Religion is therefore portrayed as essentially fatalistic and despairing:

> In the last analysis it is the theist who can find no ultimate meaning in this life and who denigrates it. For him life has no meaning *per se*. This life here and now is hopeless, barren and forlorn; it is full of tragedy and despair. The theist can only find meaning by leaving this life for a transcendental world beyond the grave. The human world as he finds it is empty of 'ultimate purpose' and hence meaningless. Theism is thus an attempt to escape from the human condition; it is a pathetic deceit (291).

But the Christian view has always been that we should develop the gifts that God has given us, as the parable of the talents in St Matthew's Gospel says, (the English use of the word 'talent' to denote mental endowment and natural abilities was actually taken from this parable). For example, Samuel Smiles wrote in the Preface to a new edition of his *Self-Help*:

> In one respect the title of the book, which it is now too late to alter, has proved unfortunate, as it has led some, who have judged it merely by the title, to suppose that it consists of a eulogy of selfishness: the very opposite of what it is, – or at least of what the author intended it to be. Although its chief object unquestionably is to stimulate youths to apply themselves diligently to right pursuits, – sparing neither labour, pains, nor self-denial in prosecuting them, – and to rely upon their own efforts in life, rather than depend on the help or patronage of others, it will also be found, from the examples given of literary and scientific men, artists, inventors, educators, philanthropists, missionaries, and martyrs, that the duty of helping one's self in the highest sense involves the helping of one's neighbours.[23]

Self-reliance here is very different from selfishness. Rather than trying to escape from the human condition, we have seen that religion gives believers reason for living hopefully and optimistically within it. Christianity has always been concerned with almsgiving, tending the sick, and with good works in general, and the best response to Kurtz's remarkable portrayal of religious fatalism and hopelessness is to refer to such Christian social reformers as Wilberforce and the Anti-Slavery campaign; Lord Shaftesbury and the factory acts, the reform of asylums, and his establishment of schools for the poor; the life of Samuel Plimsoll devoted to the welfare of merchant seamen; Dr Barnardo and his orphanages; the work of Elizabeth Fry and the Howard League for prison reform; Florence Nightingale and the revolution in nursing and public health she achieved in Britain and India and the armed services, or the YMCA and the work of the Salvation Army among the urban poor.

In Victorian Britain there were many great industrialists and entrepreneurs, especially from Quaker and Nonconformist backgrounds, who were highly successful and dynamic figures, and whose Christian beliefs were the basis of their philanthropy and generosity, not only towards their employees but the wider society. Joseph Rowntree, George Cadbury, Joseph Fry, Jesse Boot, Jeremiah Colman, William Jacob and John Carr, George Palmer, Bryant and May, W.H.Smith, W.D. and H.O.Wills, William Lever, Thomas Beecham, and William Hartley, are just some of the magnates who combined great business acumen and drive with Christian charity:

They were methodical, regular, and thrifty in their habits, relentless in their capacity for hard work and self-improvement, and models of self-discipline and temperance in their personal lifestyles... Yet although they were often extremely strict on themselves they were not puritanical killjoys who sought to condemn others to a drab life deprived of all pleasures. They were, on the contrary, cultivated and cultured men with open-minded attitudes and interests in many artistic and political movements. They also had deep warmth and compassion and determination to improve the lives of their fellow men, and particularly of those with whom they came into personal contact, not just physically but also culturally, socially, and morally. Nonconformity may have helped to make them good businessmen but it also made them humane and concerned employers and generous philanthropists. The story of the Good Samaritan carried as important a message for them as the parable of the talents.[24]

Grayling, again, claims that secular humanism in the form of the Enlightenment was the basic source of modern progress: '...it is undeniable that the two centuries that succeeded the eighteenth century saw immense advances in science, technology, education and literacy, accountable systems of government, the rule of law, and regimes of human rights; and these are the achievement of the Enlightenment' (Grayling, 144). Utilitarianism was certainly a product of the Enlightenment, and had an important influence on the social reforms of the Victorian age, but so too did Christianity, particularly in the forms of evangelical Anglicanism, Methodism, and the non-conformist churches which provided the main motivation for the various Christian reformers already referred to. Gladstone was a fervent Christian, and the Trade Union movement and the early Labour Party were strongly influenced by religious ideals, notably by Methodism[25] and by Keir Hardie, who said that the teachings of Christ had been the most important influence on his life, while we have seen that many bankers, industrialists, and entrepreneurs also tried to base their activities on Christian ethics. Many of the scientists on whose discoveries the advances in technology and industry were based were also active Christian believers, including some of the greatest such as Joseph Priestley, John Dalton, Michael Faraday and James Clerk Maxwell.

The history of Christian civilisation, in short, is filled with astonishing accomplishments in art, music, literature, science, technology, government, and every kind of benevolent social endeavour, that were not achieved despite religion, but to a significant degree because of its inspiration, and it is remarkable that our two professors can represent Christianity as fatalistic and disengaged from the world (except, of course, when busy with persecution and religious warfare).

It is true that any serious philosophy of life also has to come to terms with sorrow, disappointment, sickness, and death, with that pessimism which is a realistic and central teaching of all the world religions. For many people the world is indeed 'a vale of tears', and one of the prime functions of religion is to give hope to the hopeless. But no sensible believer would object to the enjoyment of 'the good things of life' in moderation. My Jewish dentist in Canada once said to me, 'The Rabbis teach us that at the Last Judgement we shall be asked, not just about our sins, but about the legitimate pleasures we have *failed* to enjoy', a kind of ingratitude for all the good things that God has given us.

Again, Christianity, like all the world religions warns that power, fame, and worldly success and ambition can easily become dangerous and self-destructive temptations. On the other hand it is right and proper that people should develop their abilities, and perfectly natural that they should take a legitimate pride in work well done, and applaud others for their achievements as well. Many eminent people, though quite well aware of their own achievements, are nevertheless distinguished by their modesty, and do not use them to claim superiority over others because they do not put themselves at the centre of existence.

The cartoon version of religion presented by Grayling, Kurtz, and others is no accident, because Humanists really need funda-mentalism, and as many cases of ludicrous bigotry, uncritical superstition, and slavishly literal interpretation of scriptural texts as possible, especially where they lead to violence and persecution, in order to give plausibility to their attacks on religion. Religions are supposed to be 'monolithic ideologies that say there is one great truth and one right way to live, and everyone must conform, be the same, do the same, obey, submit – that there is only one kind of good life and that it is the same for all' (Grayling, 161). It is not surprising, then, that Grayling shows marked irritation with 'non-fundamentalist religion', and with any attempt to adapt ancient teachings to modern conditions. This, 'by definition, depends on cherry-picking the given religion's doctrines, discarding the uncongenial teachings and reinterpreting the others to make them more comfortable to live with... The word that accurately and simply describes cherry-picking – choosing manageable commitments and ignoring inconvenient ones – is not a comfortable word; it is hypocrisy' (7). So, for example, was St Augustine's treatise *On the Literal Interpretation of Genesis*, referred to earlier, in which he argued that the Bible was about faith and morals, and not a science textbook, a case of 'cherry-picking hypocrisy', or was it the kind of critical thinking that has always been normal to Christianity? Anyway, moderates can safely be ignored, because 'where there are moderates, not far behind there will always be zealots' (7). Or as Dawkins says, 'The teachings of "moderate" religion, though not extremist in themselves, are an open invitation to extremism'.[26]

Far from being monolithic, Christianity, like all other religions, has actually been distracted by theological disputes throughout its history, often of the most abstruse kind. And Jesus clearly wanted his disciples to think for themselves, not to follow rules blindly: 'Once you look at the Gospels closely, it becomes apparent that inherent in the teaching of Jesus from the first was a preparedness to put accepted rules in question, where they seem harmful to human dignity and human flourishing'.[27] For example, in St Luke's Gospel, Jesus tells his disciples that unless they get rid of all their possessions, and hate their parents and their spouses and children, they cannot be His disciples. Did he mean all this quite literally, (as Grayling, no doubt, would like us to think) or was it instead a rhetorical way of shocking them into realising that they had to make God their *top* priority, and is this another example of 'cherry-picking hypocrisy', or of intelligent interpretation of a challenging passage? Deciding how the teachings of Christ are to be interpreted in daily life has always, from the first days recorded in the Gospels, required constant critical thinking.

Grayling also has a low opinion of the moral teachings of Christ in general:

> In a few respects [Jesus' teaching] is the same as all other moral systems in enjoining brotherly love and charity: that is a commonplace of any reflection on what would make for good lives and societies. But then it differs, with its own particular set of injunctions: give away all your possessions, take no thought for tomorrow (consider the lilies of the field), do not resist anyone or anything evil (turn the other cheek), obey the authorities (render unto Caesar), turn your back on your family if they disagree with you, do not marry unless you cannot contain yourself sexually... To live as a serious person in a world of many difficulties and demands, one needs something vastly richer and deeper than these anchoritic nostrums (238).

According to Grayling, who obviously takes all these command-ments quite literally, this moral teaching is thin and in practical terms unliveable and it is said to be a morality for slaves which has kept the humble in their place. 'Nothing in Judaeo-Christian ethics compares to the richness and insight of "pagan" Greek ethics, or to present-day concerns about human rights and animal rights, which are much broader, more inclusive and more sensitive than anything envisaged in religious morality' (245-6). It is interesting that John Stuart Mill, a major Humanist hero and unbeliever, took the opposite view of Christ's ethical teachings from Grayling, maintaining that they 'carry some kinds of moral goodness to a greater height than had ever been attained before'. He singles out:

> The new commandment to love one another, the recognition that the greatest are those that serve, not who are served by, others; the reverence for the weak and humble, which is the foundation of chivalry, they and not the strong being pointed out as having the first place in God's regard, and the first claim on their fellow men; the lesson of the parable of the Good Samaritan; that of 'he that is without sin let him throw the first stone'; the precept of doing as we would be done by; and such other noble moralities... (Mill 1885: 97-98)

(He argued, very strangely, that now we have discovered these moral truths, their survival no longer needs the support of religion, as though they were findings of natural science.) But why this major difference in their attitudes to Christ's moral teachings? It is surely obvious that Mill, though an unbeliever, was a product of Victorian British culture which had a profound respect for Christian values, whereas Grayling is a product of modern British culture that knows very little about Christianity and regards religion in general as weird. It is Grayling's attempt to summarise the essence of Christ's moral teaching, not Mill's, that is likely to strike us as naive and simple-minded, to say the least, and it is even more remarkable that, as a professor of philosophy, he should try to claim that modern Humanism is the intellectual descendant of the ethical teachings of Greek philosophy, and that these had nothing to say about religion. The ethical principles of Plato, Aristotle, and the later Stoics such as Seneca, Cicero, and Marcus Aurelius, and their ideas about the unique place of Man in a providentially ordered universe, were not atheist at all and were readily assimilated into Christianity together with the Old Testament. Modern Humanists are actually the intellectual heirs of the ancient atomists, who really were atheists, and did believe that the universe is meaningless and nothing more than random associations of physical particles, denigrated society, and valued only the individual and his pleasures.

Probably the favourite Humanist stereotype of religion, however, is that it has had a major responsibility for violence, warfare, and persecution throughout the ages: 'religion's terrible record of bloodshed and intolerance' (Grayling, 237). As the earlier discussion of 'the ethics of enmity' showed so clearly , it is extremely easy for human beings to generate hostility to those whom they perceive as enemies of their own community and way of life, whether they be internal heretics or external unbelievers, and the results of religious hatreds of this sort are only too well-known. Religion has also been of central importance throughout history in legitimising the claims of rulers to exercise power, so that religious orthodoxy has often become inseparably involved with loyalty to the state and with the political conflicts involved with that. This is especially true of organised religion, which has always been keen to defend its status within society and has an ignoble history of persecution for this reason. It has also been easy for the world religions, which define themselves in terms of a set of doctrinal beliefs, to quarrel with other members of their own faith over the interpretation of these doctrines. Obvious examples are Protestants and Catholics, and Sunni and Shia Muslims. But while modern religious believers are rightly ashamed of this religious warfare, (or ought to be) it is not clear why Humanists should object to it.

They are, after all, are only too keen to stress that we are just another species of animal, 'not so special after all', and as Darwinists they should realise that conflict between groups increases intra-group morale and solidarity and hence, to some degree, the inclusive fitness of its members and helps them to spread their genes. While modern Christians are likely to find the Book of Joshua, for example, morally repulsive with page after page of genocidal lunacy and slaughter, the Children of Israel presumably increased their own social solidarity, their survival chances and their inclusive fitness by exterminating large segments of the population of the Promised Land. There is no reason why a Darwinist of all people should disapprove of members of a species competing with con-specifics for living space and the material resources of milk and honey. The proper moral critique of religious fanaticism and religious wars can only come from *within* religion itself, as lamentable betrayals of its true ideals, not from biology. So while the appeal by Dawkins and other atheists to humanitarian values is no doubt perfectly sincere, it is not derived from their materialism and Darwinism at all, but from the fact that they have absorbed without realising it the traditional values of Christian civilisation in which they have been brought up.

Humanists have claimed that the world would be a much better place if religion could be made to disappear, and that atheist rationalism would provide a far superior alternative. This is a testable hypothesis, and during the twentieth century history gave immense political power to materialist, rationalist atheists in the shape of Marxist-Leninists, and allowed us to see what scientific socialism could accomplish in running society. It is rather obviously *not* the case that professedly atheist political regimes have been humane and of high moral calibre; on the contrary they have all been exceptionally brutal, corrupt, and tyrannical, based on lies and the systematic degradation of personal relations by their complete contempt for human dignity. So the Humanist, for whom reason, materialism, and atheism have up to this point been represented as the essential beacons of light for human progress, now needs to find an escape from the embarrassing fact that these crucial intellectual virtues when combined with the political power of the modern state, have led in only two or three generations to as much if not more bloodshed and suffering than religion has in the whole course of history. In order to do this, Grayling introduces the notion of 'ideology':

> ...all religions properly so called, and some philosophies, including most political philosophies, are members of a single category, the category of *ideology*. Noticing this has powerful explanatory value. The Christianity of Torquemada's Inquisition and Stalinism in the Soviet Union were both ideologies that asserted that there is one great truth, and therefore one correct way to live and behave; and that therefore everyone must sign up for it, and any deviance from it was heresy (or 'counter-revolution'), punishable even by death (Grayling, 17).

In other words, because Stalin, Chairman Mao, Pol Pot, and other Communist dictators were totalitarian and persecuted people, they had essentially become religious too! But Grayling's notion of 'ideology' is his own peculiar invention, and the word is properly defined by the leading anthropologist Dumont: 'The word "ideology" commonly designates a more or less social set of ideas and values. Thus one can speak of the ideology of a society, and also of the ideologies of more restricted groups such as a social class or movement...'.[28] There is therefore nothing necessarily totalitarian or monolithic about 'ideology' at all, and we can talk quite correctly of liberal, conservative, and socialist ideologies, for example. We shall return to the question of atheist political regimes in Chapter 4, but it is worth noting that in the form of current political correctness Humanism, too, is displaying powerful tendencies to become a persecuting orthodoxy increasingly intolerant of dissent. If Humanism does not yet do much actual persecuting, this is only because at the moment it does not have the political power to do so, but aggressive secularism is growing nevertheless, and would obviously like to impose its world-view on the rest of society if it could. This becomes especially clear in the case of human rights.

6. Human rights

When Grayling says that we need 'something vastly richer and deeper' than the teachings of Christ, he means, in particular, human rights which are the jewel in the crown of Humanism, the secular equivalent of the Gospels. Grayling and Kurtz would probably say that the importance they ascribe to human rights also shows that Humanists do feel compassion for the under-privileged after all. Proving that human rights actually exist, however, is rather more challenging: people in every country, for example, can easily discover if they have a legal right to vote, or to drive a car, but what does it mean to say that voting is a *human* right, while driving a car is not a human right (at the moment at least)? Rights based on the laws of a particular society present no problem, and a number of governments can also agree that they will all recognise, say, the right of their citizens to live in one another's territories. But what can it mean to say that individuals have certain rights simply because they are human beings, regardless of specific legislation?

One might suppose, given their emphasis on reason and evidence, that Humanists would be able to tell us exactly what methods and procedures one uses for discovering if something is or is not a human right in this sense. Humanists are notably vague about it, however, and when trying to explain why we should believe in human rights, they have nothing better to fall back on than the 'demonstrated negative effects of violating them', (Kurtz, 233), and there is '...no claim that their terms and principles were drawn from anything other than human experience, nor that their observance would get anyone into heaven. No, the claim was then, and is now, only that their observance would make this world a vastly better place' (Grayling, 183).

For religious believers, all human beings regardless of race or culture have a unique dignity and value in the scheme of things that distinguishes us from animals. This is because we have a special relationship with God, who is often compared to our Father, and to this extent as His children we all have a basic dignity and moral equality. Humanists, on the other hand, although they reject belief in God, would still like to cling on to the special status of Man:

> For example, may we not say, at minimum, that all persons are *equal*, in the sense that they are all *human*: that among the most basic of human rights is the recognition that each person has equal *dignity* and *value*; and that this ought to be respected by the world community? (Kurtz, 230)

But there is, unfortunately, no scientific basis for believing any of this: evolutionarily speaking we are just one more twig on the tree of life, and biologists are constantly reminding us that humans 'are not so special after all' but basically 'naked apes', just another species of primate. Humanists accept all this with enthusiasm: science has been 'an affront to human self-importance', showing how insignificant we are in the scheme of things. 'A non-religious ethics – a humanist ethics – is very different because it places humanity in its natural setting, with all that this implies for thinking about the good' (Grayling, 242).

It is therefore extremely odd that he and other Humanists apparently cannot see the obvious conclusion of their own materialism, which is that if humanity is just another species of animal existing in 'its natural setting' of a purely physical world, the whole idea of human rights automatically becomes meaningless and is itself a prime example of 'human self-importance'. We can have no more *value* or *significance* than ants or wasps, or any other species and, indeed, the very idea of value can have no meaning at all in a purely physical universe. According to Kurtz, 'The ethics of humanism, if it means anything, must be planetary in scope... It is the central issue of our time: how to build a global ethical consciousness' (Kurtz,194). But there is no reason in biology why belonging to the same species could be the basis of any mutual moral obligations between the members. Biologically speaking, mutual extermination between different groups of the same species would be perfectly normal as part of the struggle for survival.

The fundamental weakness of an atheist theory of human rights becomes even clearer when the claims of animal rights are brought into the argument. Professor Peter Singer, for example, maintains that 'the basic moral principle of equality' cannot be confined to our own species; we do not consider actual differences in mental or other attributes of human beings to diminish their moral equality (though many people do exactly this, as we shall see), and in the same way they are not relevant to the way in which we should treat the members of other animal species. '[T]he capacity for suffering [is] the vital characteristic that gives a being the right to equal consideration' (Singer 1989:4), and any other distinction between species is arbitrary. Regarding our species as superior is as bad as racism and sexism. On this basis, therefore, animals capable of suffering have the right not to be reared and killed for our pleasure or be experimented upon. 'It is only when we think of humans as no more than a small sub-group of all the beings that inhabit our planet that we may realise that in elevating our own species we are at the same time lowering the relative status of all other species' (7). The philosophical and theological arguments supporting a unique status for Man are peremptorily dismissed as 'these metaphysical and religious shackles' (7), but Singer obviously doesn't realise that these are the only arguments that could possibly support his case.

First of all, Singer does not tell us where his 'basic moral principle of equality' comes from: who says that all *species* are equal? Secondly, he looks at the animal kingdom exclusively from the human point of view. But if animals have moral rights, and if we are violating a mouse's rights when we torment it because it will suffer (4), then Singer should admit that cats also violate mouse rights when they eat them, and that lions, crocodiles, and sharks also violate our rights when they eat us. So either the whole process of natural selection, 'red in tooth and claw', has been one gigantic and systematic violation of animal rights but which animals are too ignorant to understand, or, the whole idea of extending the notion of rights to the natural world is simply nonsensical. This is because a system of rights, or obligations, or moral equalities is a set of values, of *ideas* that can only exist within a system of thought: one such system is human culture, and another is a meaningful cosmos ordered by God. Outside these, however, in the purely material world of nature, the notions of rights, duties, equality, and higher and lower status can make no sense at all.

Singer has subsequently agreed that it would be less misleading to talk of our obligations to animals rather than their rights, but his underlying belief in the moral equality of humans and animals remains the same: 'If an animal feels pain, the pain matters as much as it does when a human feels pain – if the pain hurts just as much and will last just as long...' (Singer 2009:156). But *matters* to whom? From the purely material point of view, which is the only one left once God is omitted, the pain of animals is irrelevant to natural selection. The evolutionary advance of the human species has been achieved by, among other things, the infliction of an enormous amount of suffering on animals, just as they have inflicted an enormous amount of suffering on each other. So what?

Treating animals as morally equal to humans is actually far more likely to trivialise the moral status of human beings than to raise the status of animals: the Christian would say, however, that denying the existence of animal rights does not condone the infliction of unnecessary suffering on them. St Francis did not need the notion of animal rights in order to show compassion to them, nor does any other religious person. If we are stewards of God's creation then animals are our fellow creatures, and believers in a God of love should obviously have compassion on animal suffering. But while there is certainly a Christian basis for compassion towards animals, there is equally certainly no case for it in biology.

Again, on the basis of biology, why should we be concerned with the well-being of other races or nations, and if the rest of the world outside our own society becomes a better place for them? Himmler put this rather well in a speech to the SS. 'One principle must be absolute for the SS man: we must be honest, decent, loyal and comradely to members of our own blood and to no one else... Whether the other peoples live in conflict or perish of hunger interests me only in so far as we need them as slaves for our culture; apart from that it does not interest me.' (Fest 1970:115)

While biologically every society needs some degree of internal solidarity if it is to survive, this provides no basis at all for the idea of individual *equality* within society, which is wholly untrue biologically, but only for winners and losers, for those who command and those who obey. Vast natural inequalities obviously exist between individual human beings in intelligence, force of personality, initiative, and ambition, and if kings and nobles, or warlords, or party apparatchiks, or business men can use their abilities to exploit the masses they are simply increasing their inclusive fitness in the approved Darwinian manner. So it should therefore be obvious at the end of all this that the doctrine of universal human rights makes as little biological sense as the doctrine of animal rights, and the only conceivable basis for human rights could be theological.

Humanists claim, however, that the doctrine of universal human rights was a triumph of rational secularism: according to Grayling (144), the rule of law and human rights in particular are achievements of the Enlightenment. This is wholly untrue. In fact the rule of law was primarily an achievement of the English-speaking peoples that began with Magna Carta. The idea of human rights to liberty and equality emerged in the context of Western Christian civilisation in the seventeenth and eighteenth centuries in the course of the ongoing debate about the divine rights of monarchy and freedom of religion. The idea of a fundamental human social equality had been familiar in the Middle Ages, and was based on our common descent from Adam and Eve: 'When Adam delved and Eve span/Who was then the gentleman?', which was the theme of the radical priest John Ball, and helped inspire the Peasants' Revolt. But the belief in human rights was also fuelled by the Protestant rebellion against the authority of the Catholic Church, and by its conception of the individual soul as in a special relationship with God, who spoke directly to the conscience of each person. This removed the need for any external moral authority, and actually made it a sin to obey such an authority if its commands offended conscience. 'A spiritual aristocrat, who sacrificed fraternity to liberty, [the Puritan] drew from his idealization of personal responsibility a theory of individual rights, which, secularized and generalized, was to be among the most potent explosives the world has known'.[29]

The assertion of political rights was also a reaction to Biblical claims for the divine right of Kings over their subjects, so the assertion of the countervailing human rights of the subjects to liberty and equality had to be derived from God as well. The argument for individual human rights to liberty, equality, and property was put forward by the seventeenth-century philosopher John Locke, and based on a hypothetical State of Nature. In this, naturally free and equal individuals roamed the land and cultivated it, but without any organised society or government. But these naturally free and equal individuals were competitive as well, so in order the better to preserve their property, personal security, and other natural rights, they came together voluntarily in a social contract and formed a state with a ruler. The social contract itself, however, could only be binding because, while these men in the state of nature were free and equal, Locke supposed that their various individual rights were derived from natural law, which itself came from God.[30]

Appealing to God via the medieval theory of natural law was an understandable tactic for getting around the Bible, but as Bertrand Russell says, very appropriately: 'The view of the state of nature and of natural law which Locke accepted from his predecessors cannot be freed from its theological basis; when it survives without this, as in much modern liberalism, it is destitute of clear logical foundation'.[31]

The Rights of Man were again promoted by Tom Paine, (*Common Sense*, 1776, and *The Rights of Man*, 1792), at the end of the eighteenth century, in the context of the struggles of the American colonists and the French against their monarchs. Paine was quite clear that God had to be the basis of universal human rights. He refers, for example, in *The Rights of Man*, to 'the divine origin of the rights of man at the creation', and to 'The illuminating and divine principle of the equal rights of man (for it has its origin from the Maker of man)...', and that 'the unity or equality' of man derives from the statement in the Bible that 'God said, Let us make man in our own image. In the image of God created He him, male and female created He them'.[32] He certainly disapproved of organised forms of religion as oppressive, and in *The Age of Reason* (1793) summed up his view of religion as 'I believe in one God, and no more; and I hope for happiness beyond this life. I believe in the equality of Man; and I believe that religious duties consist in doing justice, loving mercy, and endeavouring to make our fellow-creatures happy.'

His ideas were a very important intellectual influence in the American and French Revolutions. So the United States Declaration of Independence of 1776 stated, 'We hold these truths to be self-evident, that all men are created equal, that they are endowed by their Creator with certain inalienable Rights, that among these are Life, Liberty, and the pursuit of Happiness.' The Declaration of the Rights of Man by the French Assembly in 1789 began by saying: 'For these reasons, the National Assembly does recognise and declare, in the presence of the Supreme Being, and in the hope of his blessing and favour, the following sacred rights of men and of citizens'. The idea of human rights is therefore undeniably Christian in origin, and can be said to make *some* sense within a religious context. But human rights make no sense at all in a materialist Darwinian world, as we have seen, and their modern secularised version has degenerated into an extreme worship of the individual.

The fiction of the state of nature, in which Man was naturally an *individual*, and society a purely conventional creation, was a complete reversal of the Aristotelian view, adopted by Aquinas, that Man was naturally *social*. Aristotle was undoubtedly right, and it is quite absurd from the anthropological point of view to suppose that the human being can be represented as essentially an individual, and a society as no more than a population of individuals. As Louis Dumont has rightly said,

Our idea of society remains superficial so long as we take it, as the word suggests, as a sort of association which the fully formed individual enters voluntarily and with a definite aim, as if by a contract. Think rather of the child, slowly brought to humanity by his upbringing in the family, by the apprenticeship of language and moral judgement, by the education which makes him share in the common patrimony – including, in our society, elements which were unknown to the whole of mankind less than a century ago. Where would be the humanity of this man, where his understanding, without this training or taming, properly speaking a creation, which every society imparts to its members, by whatever actual agency? This truth is so lost from sight that it is perhaps necessary to refer our contemporaries, even if well-read, to the stories of wolf-children, so that they may reflect that individual consciousness has its source in social training.[33]

And as a matter of logic the idea of fundamental rights belonging to a lone individual outside society is also nonsense, because the only sorts of things that can belong to individuals are physical or mental qualities, like height and hair colour, or intelligence and knowledge. (It does make sense, however, to say that in the religious view dignity and value, unlike rights, can indeed attach to the individual.) The right to vote in elections, for example, or the right to own property can only exist as *institutions* within a social order and cannot conceivably attach to every individual simply as isolated human beings. But this extreme individualism of human rights, so characteristic of Western civilisation, fundamentally unbalances the relation between the individual and the social order, thereby drastically weakening the bonds of society, as we can see from these sorts of statements by human rights enthusiasts: 'The moral rights of individuals are prior to law and society... The demands of law and society derive from inherent moral rights, rather than vice versa'.[34] Or, 'Individuals have rights, and there are things no person or group may do to them (without violating their rights). So strong and far-reaching are these rights that they raise the question of what, if anything, the state and its officials may do'.[35]

It is actually quite possible to justify the rule of law and constitutional government without any appeal to human rights. In the traditional view of kingship in more or less all societies, and certainly in Christian civilisation, it was held that while the king was ordained or legitimated by divine authority, he in turn had obligations to his subjects, in particular to rule them justly, to maintain order, and protect the weak from the strong. In the British Coronation Oath, for example, monarchs promise before God to cause Law and Justice, in Mercy, to be executed in all their judgements. In the pre-modern world the main political problem, of course, was to get rulers to honour their obligations to their subjects. We in the West have inherited the same tradition, and naturally approve of the rule of law and constitutional government that were first developed, not by Humanists but by the Christian English-speaking world from Magna Carta onwards. Within this context it is perfectly reasonable to say that the state exists for the good of the people and to preserve order and justice, but that because power corrupts, there should be certain institutional restraints on government that we now refer to as the rule of law and constitutional government. These are embodied in a number of political rights, or 'civil liberties' that specifically target those areas where oppressive governments are most likely to attack their citizens: rights such as freedom of speech and of the press, security of one's person, home, and possessions from arbitrary search or seizure, to communicate freely with others and assemble peacefully without surveillance by the state, the right of the people to hold the government to account in elections, freedom from torture, and the right to a fair trial, and not to be imprisoned indefinitely without one. Since atheists, however, must reject the divine origins of the state's duties to its citizens, it is hard to see why they could have any principled objection to tyranny. So Nietzsche argued quite consistently that in a society ruled by superior beings, the duty of the inferior masses is to serve them.

But while political rights can be fairly clearly and tightly defined in terms of the duties of governments to their citizens, the idea of human rights has been expanded to embrace what can be called social rights, and it is here that the anti-social nature of human rights really becomes obvious. We now find a much broader type of individual human right that is not concerned so much with what governments should *refrain* from doing, as with what society as a whole, and indeed the whole human race, *ought* to do for those who are seen as oppressed in a vast number of different ways. The problem with these broader social rights is to discover how to decide that each one exists, and then how to balance them against all the other requirements of social life – public order and health, the needs of the economy and industry, administrative efficiency and so on. 'Rights are trumps', as the legal theorist Richard Dworkin has put it, and so all other considerations of a well-ordered society have to give way to these assertions of self-interest.

The Universal Declaration of Human Rights by the United Nations lists some of these: the right to have a job, to family life, to rest and leisure, to education, and to enjoy the arts, for example, and the Olympic Charter says that sport is also a human right. In this conception of human rights we are no longer dealing with the victims of oppression by governments, but with what are portrayed as the victims of society, or of life in general, and who are said to have had a raw deal. No one would deny that having a job, being able to marry and have a family, to receive an education, to enjoy the arts and sport, and so on are all good things. But unlike political rights, where there are rational criteria for discussing, say, the right to vote, to freedom of expression, or the criteria of a fair trial; social rights are simply a wish list of nice things that people would like to have or to do, to which one could go on adding indefinitely: the right to a good standard of living, to be included in the life of one's community, to a stable future, to have access to broadband, to be famous, and, of course, the American right to the pursuit of happiness.

If these secular human rights were no more than a wish list of the good things in life they would be harmless enough. But the idea of a 'right' means that if I don't get what I want on my wish list, someone is to *blame*: they have violated my rights and must be made to pay. This inflames a sense of grievance against society and encourages individuals to adopt the posture of victim, even where no one is to blame and nothing practical can be done. The cult of victimhood has distorted our social perceptions to the extent that we are now on the verge of accepting a right not to be offended by other people's opinions, under the guise of preventing harassment or creating a 'safe space'. These general social rights have therefore become the basis of a whole new culture of entitlement without any corresponding sense of social responsibility and duty, and as we shall see in the next chapter, entitlement is closely linked to narcissism.

For example, a few years ago a case was brought in Ontario by a woman who claimed the fundamental human right to walk about in public bare-breasted because men were allowed to, and the prohibition on women doing this was therefore gender discrimination. The Supreme Court of Ontario subsequently ruled in her favour. Or, notoriously, foreign criminals, convicted of the most serious offences in Britain, have repeatedly been able to avoid deportation by appealing to the European Charter of Human Rights that their right to a family life would be violated if they were separated from their partners or children acquired while in this country.

Human rights have also become group as well as individual rights. The prototype of group rights was Marx's depiction of the oppression of the working class by their capitalist employers, but this basic idea of group rights was inflated in the twentieth century by the Marxist Gramsci and his notion of 'hegemony'. This means the domination of society not just by violence or economic power, but by the outlook and standards of the bourgeoisie, which the workers are duped into accepting as common sense values for everybody. Those who are intellectually enlightened, however, can liberate the downtrodden by showing them how they are being culturally oppressed.

So we have now gone far beyond the simple idea of a

government potentially tyrannising its citizens, and society itself has been steadily transformed into a vast system of oppression, not just of workers, but of blacks and all ethnic minorities, of women, of homosexuals, of transsexuals, of the disabled, of the overweight, of the ugly, of the less intelligent, of children, and so on and on, all of whom form 'communities' with their separate grievances. Their oppressors are basically white, Western heterosexual males determined to preserve their power and keep capitalist, imperialist, colonialist, sexist, and classist systems in place. The obvious outcome is a society permeated by increasing rage and resentment as more and more 'communities' are persuaded that they should consider themselves as victims.

Logic is a tool of male domination, and the male emphasis on the dispassionate mastery of facts and rigorous critical thinking is compared unfavourably with women's forms of knowing, emphasising common experience and shared feelings. The concept of intellectual merit is also often viewed with suspicion as offensively masculine, competitive, and a threat to communal harmony and universal self-esteem.[36] Again, societies have traditionally regarded children's education as requiring a level of discipline that would be inappropriate for adults, including physical punishment. But advocates of children's rights regard discipline in schools as a violation of children's rights, and not just discipline but teaching itself is now being represented as a form of oppression because it prevents children discovering their true identities. Indeed, the very idea of normality is seen as oppressive because it stigmatises anyone who is different from bourgeois standards. It is the offence of 'Ableism': 'Ableism is the heresy that normal physical, mental, and emotional behavior is beneficial. Research evidence supports an opposing conclusion, that equating normal with desirable is disparaging and potentially harmful to disabled persons.' 'Healthism', or encouraging people to watch their health, is a similar heresy, 'a coercive and potentially fascist act linked to capitalism, racism, and Nazi-style eugenics'.[37] So Diet Soda, for example, is oppressive to fat people because it carries an implicit criticism of their excessive weight. 'Fat acceptance campaigners raise concerns that modern culture's concern with weight loss may not have a foundation in scientific research, but instead is an example of using science as a means to control deviance, as a part of society's attempt to deal with something that it finds disturbing'.[38] But there are many other 'communities' as well, such as '...those deaf identity advocates who argue that to eliminate deafness would be a genocidal assault on a language community' ...'the "Mad Pride" movement which encourages schizophrenics to refuse medication and revel in their condition' ...[and] ...'the "Pro-Ana" websites that encourage anorexics to celebrate their identity by starving themselves to death'.[39]

While the human rights of every sort of aggrieved and vocal minority are being defended against conformity to legal and social norms, there is an equally obvious tendency to remove human rights from the most defenceless members of society, those at the beginning and end of their lives. The basic argument here is not, however, the capacity for suffering, but the entirely different assumption that human life as such is not valuable, and only life of a certain intellectual quality entitles someone to claim to be a person. This is a fatal concession which at once opens the door to contempt rather than compassion for the weak, who can now become regarded as sub-human or 'surplus to requirements'. For example, two medical 'ethicists' have recently argued that it should be permissible to kill the newborn as well as foetuses because they are not 'persons' having a moral right to life, 'that is, the point at which they will be able to make aims and appreciate their own life':

> If a potential person, like a fetus and a newborn, does not become an actual person, like you and us [the authors], then there is neither an actual nor a future person who can be

harmed, which means that there is no harm at all. So, if you ask one of us if we would have been harmed, had our parents decided to kill us when we were fetuses or newborns, our answer is 'no', because they would have harmed someone who does not exist, (the 'us' whom you are asking the question), which means no one. And if no one is harmed, then no harm has occurred.[40]

But while one can debate the meaning of 'person', they are still little *human lives*, little *human beings*, and the distinction between 'potential' and 'actual' persons cannot alter this: to say that no harm is being done, and they are only 'uterine contents', really indicates an astonishing lack of imagination. If a botanist had the last surviving seed in the world of a species of tree, and suggested throwing it on the fire, would we think this quite trivial: 'he's not harming anything really because it's only a potential tree'? Or would we be outraged and say that quibbling about potential versus actual trees was irrelevant, and that he was cutting off a life full of interest and possibilities before it had had a chance to develop? I rather think the second response would be more likely, because we *value* the prospect of the potential tree. And if a woman discovers that she is expecting a baby, her normal and *rational* reaction is to be happy and excited at the prospect of her child's arrival, of bringing a new person into the world with the precious gift of life. We don't tell her that she is being irrational because nothing of any moral importance is actually there at the moment. Indeed, if the foetus really has no moral significance why should the mother refrain from alcohol or other practices that medically endanger it? And if she drinks recklessly and her baby is born with foetal alcohol syndrome, why has she done anything morally wrong?

If foetuses and newborns simply don't exist as persons and are morally irrelevant, then the reasons for killing them can be correspondingly trivial: '...if economical, social or psychological circumstances change such that taking care of the offspring becomes an unbearable burden on someone, then people should be given the chance of not being forced to do something they cannot afford'.[41] The burden doesn't in fact have to be unbearable at all, so that the cost to the state of bringing up Down's Syndrome children, even if they are happy, is said to justify their extermination. In the same way, Alzheimer's patients or other victims of dementia beyond a certain stage, who can no longer formulate coherent aims in their lives, have obviously ceased to be 'persons' too, and killing them does no harm at all and relieves us of all the trouble and expense of looking after them and their filthy habits. Indeed, those below a certain minimum IQ might also come to be regarded as 'non-persons', and with a little effort we might extend this principle to unemployables who are another massive drain on the economy, and so on. But the greatest burden on the economy are the growing numbers of the elderly, and utopian thinkers have often speculated about the advantages of bringing an end to their lives before nature takes its course. In the modern liberal age, of course, we would not talk about anything so crude as extermination but rather of Dying with Dignity. This really sounds rather appealing, and not only as a last resort for those in extreme suffering but something so easily converted into a duty, the final contribution that the elderly can be asked to make to the GDP.

Others argue that, just as some human lives, like infants, and the unborn, and geriatrics, have no moral value because they do not qualify as 'persons', *some* animal lives do have moral value on this basis, and favourite candidates are chimpanzees and bonobos. (Dolphins have also been included in the list of non-human persons, but since recent research[42] has shown that their intelligence is actually not very different from that of chickens, their place on the list now seems rather tenuous or, on second thoughts, chickens' rights may have to be re-evaluated.)

The idea that rights are automatically conferred by the

possession of some degree of intelligence has led to increasing discussion of when the concept of universal rights will be extended to robots. In recent research, commissioned by the UK Office of Science and Innovation's Horizon Scanning Centre, a paper on 'Robo-rights: Utopian dream or rise of the machines?' (2006), examines the developments in artificial intelligence and their possible effects on law and politics. It says a 'monumental shift' could occur if robots develop to the point where they can reproduce, improve themselves or develop artificial intelligence. The research concludes that in the next 20 to 50 years robots could be granted rights. If this happened, the robots would have certain responsibilities such as voting, the obligation to pay taxes, and perhaps performing compulsory military service, while society would also have a duty of care for these new digital citizens. This *reductio ad absurdum* seems a fitting conclusion to our exploration of the moral riches of human rights.

7. Humanism and WEIRD societies

For the anthropologist, one of the most striking features of Humanists like Grayling and Kurtz is that, despite being philosophers and despite the emphasis they place on each person thinking for him or herself, they assume quite uncritically and ethnocentrically that the Western secular liberal view of society and individual rights is self-evident and unchallengeable for the whole human race, without realising how eccentric it is in the world context. The social psychologist Jonathan Haidt has described our Western societies as WEIRD, that is, Western, Educated, Industrialised, Rich, and Democratic:

> WEIRD people are statistical outliers; they are the least typical, least representative, people you could study if you want to make generalizations about human nature. Even within the West, Americans are more extreme outliers than Europeans, and within the United States, the educated upper

middle class is the most unusual of all. Several of the peculiarities of WEIRD culture can be captured in this simple generalization: *The WEIRDer you are, the more you see a world full of separate objects, rather than relationships.*[43]

Societies like ours, with their worship of the individual, will therefore have a distinctive brand of moral thought: '...it makes sense that WEIRD philosophers since Kant and Mill have mostly generated moral systems that are individualistic, rule-based, and universalist. That's the morality you need to govern a society of autonomous individuals'.[44] Individual rights focusing on *fairness* and *harm* then take centre stage; to paraphrase Mill, 'it doesn't matter what you do as long as it doesn't harm anyone else'; while the idea of duty becomes increasingly regarded as oppressive and censorious – 'who are you to tell me what I ought to do?'

In the traditions of other civilisations, and in Christian Europe before the Reformation, the social or moral order comes first, however:

The ethic of *community* is based on the idea that people are, first and foremost, members of larger entities such as families, teams, armies, companies, tribes, and nations. These larger entities are more than the sum of the people who compose them; they are real, they matter, and they must be protected. People have an obligation to play their assigned roles in these entities. Many societies therefore develop moral concepts such as duty, hierarchy, respect, reputation, and patriotism. In such societies, the Western insistence that people should design their own lives and pursue their own goals seems selfish and dangerous – a sure way to weaken the social fabric and destroy the institutions and collective entities upon which everyone depends.[45]

Religion has always been an integral and traditional part of the ethics of community, as so defined, reinforcing the idea of the sanctity of institutions and the dignity of the individual:

> The ethic of *divinity* is based on the idea that people are, first and foremost, temporary vessels within which a divine soul has been implanted. People are not just animals with an extra helping of consciousness: they are children of God and should behave accordingly. The body is a temple, not a playground. Even if it does no harm and violates nobody's rights when a man has sex with a chicken carcase, he still shouldn't do it because it degrades him, dishonors his creator, and violates the sacred order of the universe. Many societies therefore develop moral concepts such as sanctity and sin, purity and pollution, elevation and degradation. In such societies, the personal liberty of secular Western nations looks like libertinism, hedonism, and a celebration of humanity's baser instincts.[46]

Many peoples therefore regard the attempts by secular Western liberalism to make the whole world adopt its values, and especially human rights, as cultural arrogance. Humanism has no answer to religious ethics because, despite all its talk of reason and evidence and thinking for oneself its exponents make no attempt to provide a scholarly analysis of religion or ethics or evolutionary biology, but are happy to take the undemanding route of endorsing the fashionable values of modern Western liberalism.

Chapter 4

Some Atheist Utopias

Humanism has an obvious appeal to Westerners simply because it is an ethnocentric defence of their own culture of liberal individualism and consumerism. But now we come to a variety of philosophies that, like Humanism, absolutely reject the spiritual dimension of existence but would like to reconstruct society on more rigorously atheist and materialist principles. Dawkins asks '...whether atheism systematically influences people to do bad things. There is not the smallest evidence that it does'.[1] As individuals, atheists can of course be decent and honourable people but that is not the real point: this is, what sorts of *public moralities* are likely to be encouraged by the materialistic, Darwinian world-view on which modern atheism is based? Contrary to Dawkins we have already noted plenty of evidence for the part that atheism played in the various Communist tyrannies of the twentieth century, and now we can explore in more detail the inherently anti-human tendencies of scientific rationalism and materialism, in which we shall find that Darwinian ideas keep recurring, and that there is an extreme hostility to religion in general and to Christianity in particular.

If matter is the only reality and we are simply another species of animal, an accidental by-product of the evolutionary process, any secular system of ethics will inherently tend to go in one of two main directions. The first is the belief that only the individual is real and society is just a population of competing individuals, all of whom are free to pursue their own interests. The case of the ancient atomists showed that these will almost inevitably be oriented towards worldly success, greed, and pleasure – after all, if this world is the only one, what else is left? This has an obvious appeal to the individualist cultures of the English-speaking world, in particular, as opposed to the second type of system, which is based on the belief that society is the primary reality and itself creates the individual. The state, as the institutional expression of society as a whole, is then likely to become the dominant agency through which progress can be achieved, and only through participation in this can individuals find any meaning and purpose in their lives. The social order itself therefore assumes supreme importance while the individual has none. But there is another variation on this: the biologistic view that the human race is radically unequal in the struggle for survival, that natural leaders are inherently superior to the masses, and that the state can be used by its ruler merely as a tool for oppression and conquest. So let us first see where radical individualism takes us.

1. Objectivism

In the late nineteenth century, so-called 'Social Darwinism' advocated ruthless individualism[2] and unrestricted economic competition, as part of the general theory of evolution. The most influential modern representative of this tradition has been the late Ayn Rand, an extremely popular American social theorist who founded the ethical doctrine known as Objectivism and which is still propagated by the Ayn Rand Institute. She was an immigrant to the United States from Russia where she had seen her father's business and fortune confiscated by the Communist revolutionaries. Not surprisingly she became a passionate advocate for pure, unbridled capitalism and one of the most influential social and ethical thinkers of modern times who included many prominent Americans among her admirers. She named her philosophy 'Objectivism' because it is said to be based on reason and science, whereas mere hedonism is irresponsible and irrational, and guided only by emotion and desires. Her principal disciple and for a time her lover was Nathaniel Branden, who contributed some of the chapters in *The*

Virtue of Selfishness (1964) from which the following quotations are taken. After breaking up with her, in 1969 he published *The Psychology of Self-Esteem*, which was the first popular psychology book promoting what has become the Self-Esteem Movement in the United States, (and to which we shall return in more detail later).

According to Objectivism people are born as blank slates: 'The foundation and starting point of man's thinking are his sensory perceptions' (Rand 1964:42), and 'Reason is the faculty that identifies and integrates the material provided by man's senses' (22). Thus the individual is the rock-bottom reality: '...there is no such thing as 'society', since society is only a number of individual men' (15) so, logically, 'An organism's life is its standard of value: that which furthers its life is the *good*, that which threatens it is the *evil*' (17). 'The basic social principle of the Objectivist ethics is that just as life is an end in itself, so every living human being is an end in himself, not the means to the ends or the welfare of others – and, therefore, that man must live for his own sake, neither sacrificing himself to others, nor sacrificing others to himself. To live for his own sake means that *the achievement of his own happiness is man's highest moral purpose*' (30).

The basis of happiness for the rational man is his work: 'Productive work is the central purpose of a rational man's life, the central value that integrates and determines the hierarchy of all his other values. Reason is the source, the precondition of his productive work – pride is the result' (27). Pride, self-esteem, and success are fundamental values in Objectivism: 'In order to deal with reality successfully – to pursue and achieve the values which his life requires – man needs self-esteem: he needs it to be confident of his efficacy and worth' (40). Anxiety and guilt are symptoms of mental illness because they are produced by a sense of impotence, whereas pride in one's success is an indication of mental health as a result of one's control over reality. (Some strong resemblances to Humanism are obvious here.)

Rand is of course aware that her radically selfish individuals have nevertheless to co-operate, and says that it is a basic principle of Objectivist ethics that no one may use physical force against another except in self-defence, and must respect the rights of others as they must respect his. 'Individualism regards man, every man, as an independent, sovereign entity who possesses an inalienable right to his own life, a right derived from his nature as a rational being. Individualism holds that a civilized society, or any form of association, co-operation, or peaceful co-existence among men, can be achieved only on the basis of individual rights – and that a group as such, has no rights other than the individual rights of its members' (150). Government is necessary, but its only purpose is to defend individual rights central to which is the right to own property: 'No human rights can exist without property rights... if the producer does not own the result of his effort, he does not own his own life' (106). It is worth noting, however, that neither she nor Branden make any serious philosophical attempt to prove the existence of these inalienable individual rights, or explain how they have been arrived at. Why, for example, should rights be the conditions of man's existence that he needs to survive (111) when most societies have survived quite well without them? Again, the claim that we are independent sovereign entities simply because we are rational beings does not follow, and ignores the obvious fact that we are only rational because we are also social, and could only have developed our minds within human society.

In the Objectivist view, capitalism, 'full, pure, uncontrolled, unregulated, laissez-faire capitalism' is the only truly ethical system because only capitalism is based on justice. 'The principle of *trade* is the only rational ethical principle for *all human relationships* [my emphasis], personal and social, private and public, spiritual [pertaining to consciousness], and material. It is the principle of justice' (34). Capitalism is not only the supreme manifestation of justice, but it offers unique opportunities for personal success and achievement: 'Life is growth; not to move forward is to fall backward... Every step upward opens to man a wider range of activity and achievement... The great merit of capitalism is its unique appropriateness to... man's need to grow. Leaving men free to think, to act, to produce, to attempt the untried and the new, its principles operate in a way that rewards effort and achievement, and penalizes passivity' (142-3).

On the other hand, Rand has the utmost contempt for altruism. It is 'the ethical theory which regards man as a sacrificial animal, which holds that man has no right to exist for his own sake, that service to others is the only justification of his existence, and that self-sacrifice is the highest moral duty, virtue, and value' (37-8). 'My views on charity are very simple. I do not consider it a major virtue and, above all, I do not consider it a moral duty. There is nothing wrong in helping other people, if and when they are worthy of the help and you can afford to help them. I regard charity as a marginal issue. What I am fighting is the idea that charity is a moral duty and a primary virtue'(Playboy, March 1964). Love itself is a form of selfishness: 'One gains a profoundly personal, selfish joy from the mere existence of the person one loves. It is one's own personal, selfish happiness that one seeks, earns and derives from love' (51). On risking one's own life to save others, she says 'If the person to be saved is a stranger, then it is proper to take only minimal risk to save him or her', and if it is a loved one, 'there one can be willing to give one's own life to save him or her for the selfish reason that life without the loved person can be unbearable' (52). Rather the same argument could be advanced for an alcoholic trying to save a crate of his favourite whisky.

If marriage, on this basis, is therefore problematic, Objectivists, rather understandably, have virtually nothing to say about the obligations of parents to their children. Ayn Rand herself was apparently too busy to have any, and scarcely refers to them in her writings, but the only apparent reason why an Objectivist would have children without falling into the trap of self-sacrifice would surely be as investments. But if such children, on the other hand, had absorbed true Objectivist principles, as sovereign individuals they should rightly resist being treated as a means to someone else's ends. Not, one would suppose, much of a recipe for a happy family life. Nor can one see any reason why Objectivists would be foolish enough to risk their lives fighting for their country, and the best that Ayn Rand could do, in an address to West Point Military Academy, on military service, was to dress it up as a form of self-defence:

> You have chosen to risk your lives for the defense of this country. I will not insult you by saying that you are dedicated to selfless service – it is not a virtue in my morality. In my morality, the defense of one's country means that a man is personally unwilling to live as the conquered slave of any enemy, foreign or domestic. This is an enormous virtue. Some of you may not be consciously aware of it. I want to help you realize it.[3]

It will hardly be surprising from all this that Objectivism abominates religion as a perverse celebration of irrationality, impotence, and worldly failure, a product of mental illness. According to Nathaniel Branden:

> Faith is a malignancy that no system can tolerate with impunity; and the man who succumbs to it, will call on it in precisely those issues where he needs his reason most. When one turns from reason to faith, when one rejects the absolutism of reality, one undercuts the absolutism of one's consciousness – and one's mind becomes an organ one cannot trust any longer. It becomes what the mystics claim it to be: a tool of distortion.[4]

The religious emphasis on humility and its refusal to give priority to worldly values and success is particularly offensive:

> If it is a virtue to renounce one's mind, but a sin to use it; if it is a virtue to approximate the mental state of a schizophrenic, but a sin to be in intellectual focus; if it is a virtue to denounce this earth, but a sin to make it liveable; if it is a virtue to despise life, but a sin to sustain and enjoy it – then no self-esteem, or control or efficacy are possible to man, *nothing* is possible to him but the guilt and terror of a wretch caught in a nightmare universe, a universe created by some metaphysical sadist who has cast man into a maze where the door marked 'virtue' leads to self-destruction and the door marked 'efficacy' leads to self-damnation.[5]

As already noted, Branden wrote an important book promoting the psychological necessity of self-esteem, but this has subsequently been increasingly criticised: claims for the importance of self-esteem for personal well-being are now held to be grossly exaggerated, and it has been noted that there is a significant tendency for self-esteem to become narcissism: 'In normal populations, scores in the Narcissistic Personality Inventory... correlate substantially with self-esteem'.[6] Narcissists are remarkably obnoxious people, as the Narcissistic Personality Inventory makes clear, with a significant resemblance to psychopaths.[7] Their defining characteristics are:

1. A grandiose sense of one's self-importance.
2. Pre-occupation with fantasies of unlimited success, power, brilliance, beauty, or ideal love.
3. Exhibitionism.
4. Responding to criticism, indifference, or defeat either with cool indifference or with marked feelings of rage, inferiority, shame, humiliation, or emptiness.

5. Entitlement, expecting special favours without assuming reciprocal responsibilities.
6. Exploitativeness.
7. Relationships vacillate between the extremes of over-idealization and devaluation.
8. Lack of empathy.

The trend to a narcissistic culture of self-love and entitlement really took off in America in the 1970s, in company with the self-esteem movement, and as we all know, what first appears there soon tends to spread to the rest of the world, especially the West:

> Understanding the narcissism epidemic is important because its long-term consequences are destructive to society. American culture's focus on self-admiration has caused a flight from reality to the land of grandiose fantasy. We have phony rich people (with interest-only mortgages and piles of debt), phony beauty (with plastic surgery and cosmetic procedures), phony athletes (with performance-enhancing drugs), phony celebrities (via reality TV and YouTube), phony genius students (with grade inflation), a phony national economy (with $11 trillion of government debt), phony feelings of being special among children (with parenting and education focused on self-esteem), and phony friends (with the social networking explosion). All this fantasy might feel good, but, unfortunately, reality always wins. The mortgage meltdown and the resulting financial crisis are just one demonstration of how inflated desires eventually crash to earth (Twenge and Campbell 2009:4).

In fact, as they conclude, 'Narcissism causes almost all of the things that Americans hoped that high self-esteem would prevent, including aggression, materialism, lack of caring for others, and shallow values' (9). A number of obvious cultural factors have fertilised the growth of narcissism, in particular: the enormous growth of television and the entertainment industry, with its cult of celebrity and materialism; easy credit allowing us to have what we want *now*; the Internet with Facebook, Twitter, YouTube, MySpace, and other social networking sites that pander to personal vanity; and the school system with its basic belief that every child must constantly be told that it is special and never criticised regardless of its actual achievements.

Another major factor is wealth. We know that Jesus, like just about every other religious teacher, took a dim view of the rich and thought the poor were generally better people, and modern sociology supports this. For example, 'Upper class individuals are more prone to feelings of entitlement and narcissistic tendencies', whereas 'Lower-class individuals are more likely to spend time taking care of others, and they are more embedded in social networks that depend on mutual aid'.[8] 'Individuals from upper-class backgrounds are also less generous and altruistic... upper-class individuals are particularly likely to value their own welfare over the welfare of others and, thus, may hold more positive attitudes toward greed'.[9] It is for these obvious reasons that greed, like pride, has always been a deadly sin in all the world religions.

Anthropologically, the Objectivist dismissal of society as unreal is complete nonsense: individuals only become human through their membership of society, and the Objectivist notion of individual human rights is nonsense too, based on a philosophical muddle that we have already explored in the previous chapter. Notably, Objectivism rather obviously does not lead to human happiness, and cannot even deal with such basic moral situations as marriage and the family, or friendship. Being a good neighbour is problematic, any voluntary public service is generally to be avoided, while actually risking one's life as a fireman or fighting for one's country in a real war would be insane, although it also has to be conceded that Objectivists would not engage in political tyranny.

Most Utopian schemes, however, are distinctly hostile to individualism as such, let alone an extreme version like Objectivism, because they consider it to be inherently irrational and a basic obstacle to the scientifically planned society, which is the only way of building paradise on earth. While Objectivists claim to base their ideas exclusively on reason and science, the candid reader of their works will see at once that these ideas are essentially philosophical and anecdotal, and not based on the usual types of biological and sociological evidence and least of all on experiment.

2. Skinner's Behaviourist utopia

The American Behaviourist Professor B.F.Skinner, often described as the most influential psychologist since Freud, believed that a genuine science of human behaviour had to be experimental and follow exactly the same rigorously materialistic methods as physics and biology. If this were done, he claimed, it would be possible to design perfect human communities free of all the conflicts and emotional disturbances that hitherto have plagued human existence.

We remember from Chapter 1 that Skinner regarded belief in the mind as a superstitious fantasy because it is obviously impossible for a mental event to cause a physical one, and he claimed that modern believers in the mind are like primitive animists who think physical objects can be inhabited by spirits. As he said in a book actually called 'Beyond Freedom and Dignity', we must dismiss the whole idea of the mind, consciousness, thought, and the belief in free will and human dignity, and instead 'follow the path taken by physics and biology by turning directly to the relation between behaviour and the environment and neglecting supposed mediating states of mind'.[10]

Skinner regarded experiment as the only path to understanding human behaviour, and he was particularly contemptuous of the belief that we can learn anything from history about how to attain happiness, because history was an unanalysable mess from which no scientific conclusions about the conditions of happiness could be drawn: 'What did we know about happiness anyway? Had there ever been enough of it in the world in any one spot and at any one time for a decent experiment?'[11]

According to Skinner, the environment shapes us in two fundamental ways – through our biological inheritance by natural selection, and through the positive and negative reinforcement our behaviour receives from other people and the physical world. 'A person does not act on the world, the world acts upon him'.[12] While he believed that the relative importance of heredity and environment had to be decided by experiment, he tended to minimize the importance of heredity, and was in no doubt that not only are we are entirely material so that the mind is an illusion, but are also entirely passive to external influences.

What is being abolished is autonomous man – the inner man, the homunculus, the possessing demon, the man defended by the literature of freedom and dignity. This abolition has long been overdue... He has been constructed from our ignorance, and as our understanding increases, the very stuff of which he is composed vanishes. Science does not dehumanize man, it de-homunculizes him, and it must do so if it is to prevent the abolition of the human species. To man *qua* man we readily say good riddance. Only by dispossessing him can we turn to the real causes of human behavior. Only then can we turn from the inferred to the observed, from the miraculous to the natural, from the inaccessible to the manipulable. It is often said that in doing so we must treat the man who survives as a mere animal. 'Animal' is a pejorative term, but only because 'man' has been made spuriously honorific. Krutch has argued that whereas the traditional view supports Hamlet's exclamation, 'How like a god!', Pavlov, the behavioral scientist, emphasized 'How like a dog!' But that was a step forward. A god is an archetypal pattern of an explanatory fiction, of a miracle-working mind, of the metaphysical. Man is much more than a dog, but like a dog he is within range of a scientific analysis.[13]

I have quoted this magnificent rant at some length because it gives such a clear view of Skinner's idea of Man. His basic research was conducted on rats and pigeons in highly controlled experimental conditions in a laboratory. It focused on 'operant', or voluntary, behaviour as opposed to the reflex behaviour studied by earlier researchers such as Pavlov, and on how operant behaviour could be modified by different programmes of conditioning, or 'schedules of reinforcement'. The animal is placed in a box with a bar attached to one wall so that when the bar is pressed a food pellet is dropped into a tray. The stimulus of the food pellet is said to 'positively reinforce' the strength of the bar-pressing response, that is, make it more likely that the bar will be pressed again. (Pigeons peck at different coloured discs on the wall instead of pressing the bar, while cats refuse to take part at all.) If the release of the pellet is then made to depend, say, on a light flashing, as well as on a bar-press, the rat learns to press the bar only when the light is on. This sort of response is said to be under the 'stimulus control' of the light. On the other hand, we can change the behaviour of a laboratory animal, not by rewarding a certain response with a food pellet, but by discouraging it by something unpleasant like an electric shock. Positive reinforcement therefore involves reward; negative reinforcement involves the avoidance of something unpleasant.

The behaviour of rats and pigeons can be modified in very elaborate ways by different programmes of conditioning, or 'schedules of reinforcement'. But it must be emphasised that Skinner does not regard reinforcement as causing good or bad *feelings*, which then modify our behaviour, because feelings themselves are part of that inner man whom Skinner is so keen to banish. Feelings are not the causes of behaviour, but the by-products of it, so 'we do not run away because we are afraid: we are afraid because we run away'(17)! To admit the causal power of feelings would be to admit that internal states can be causes, whereas it is the behaviour that is selected by reinforcement, not the feelings: 'We pull our hand away from a hot object, but not because the object feels painful. The behavior occurs because appropriate mechanisms have been selected in the course of evolution. The feelings are merely collateral products of the conditions responsible for the behavior' (Skinner 1974:47).

Similarly, memories are not stored internally in our heads – they are simply changes in the probability of our behaviour: 'Techniques of recall are not concerned with searching a store-house of memory, but with increasing the probability of a response' (109-110).

The idea that our behaviour can be modified by trial and error and by positive and negative consequences is, of course, quite true and familiar, and Skinner added various refinements to this, such as the greater effectiveness of positive reinforcement over negative reinforcement in improving behaviour. But it has always been obvious to the many critics of Behaviourism that while 'units of behaviour', 'stimulus', 'response', and 'schedules of reinforcement' can be given precise definitions in the context of laboratory experiments, the case is utterly different in real life situations in human society.

The problems of transferring behaviourist terminology from the laboratory to the real world became particularly obvious when Skinner tried to treat language as 'verbal behavior', an enterprise that was devastatingly refuted[14] by the eminent professor of linguistics, Noam Chomsky, in his review of Skinner's book *Verbal Behavior*. Skinner could not of course admit that speech conveyed thoughts, so had to maintain that its only distinctive feature was that it affected *people* as opposed to things. But this did nothing to rescue his explanatory concepts from their inherent vagueness. So, for example, is a political party's promise to give a tax-cut to people in my income-bracket a stimulus, and is my vote for them at the next election a response under the stimulus control of the properties of 'tax-cut'? But suppose I do *not* vote for them, perhaps because I am disgusted by such a flagrant attempt to buy my vote. Then my voting for another party would be explained as a response under the stimulus control of the properties of 'bribery', and so on indefinitely. As Chomsky says,

> A typical example of 'stimulus control' for Skinner would be the response to a piece of music with the utterance *Mozart* or to a painting with the response *Dutch*. These responses are asserted to be 'under the control of extremely subtle properties' of the physical object or event. Suppose that instead of saying Dutch we had said *Clashes with the wallpaper, I thought you liked abstract work, Never saw it before, Tilted, Hanging too low, Beautiful, Hideous, Remember our camping trip last summer?*, or whatever else might come into our minds when looking at a picture (in Skinnerian translation, whatever other responses exist in sufficient strength). Skinner could only say that each of these responses is under the control of some other stimulus property of the physical object.[15]

So, unlike in the laboratory, we can only identify the relevant stimulus *after* we have already heard the response. In these kinds of situation which are entirely typical of ordinary life we can see that the very notion of 'stimulus' has obviously lost all meaning.

The same objection applies to Skinner's very important idea of self-reinforcement. So, 'a man talks to himself ...because of the reinforcement he receives', and 'Just as the musician plays or composes what he is reinforced by hearing, or as the artist paints what reinforces him visually, so the speaker engaged in verbal fantasy says what he is reinforced by hearing or what he is reinforced by reading'.[16] 'Self-reinforcement' therefore turns out to be just as empty an explanation of real human behaviour as 'stimulus'.

Behaviourism can therefore tell us little about actual human behaviour while ethics, as traditionally understood, clearly has no place at all in Skinner's thought. The autonomous individual at the centre of ethics no longer exists, and all that is left is a shell that is 'at best a repertoire of behaviors imparted by an organized set of contingencies'[17], and since free will is an illusion, the 'goodness' produced by operant conditioning must in a sense be quite automatic. That is, without the necessary social conditioning from infancy we are not spontaneously altruistic, or compassionate, or co-operative, or public-spirited at all.

Skinner conceives good and bad basically in terms of adaptation and survival:

There are remarkable similarities in natural selection, operant conditioning, and the evolution of social environments. Not only do all three dispense with a prior creative design and a prior purpose, they invoke the notion of survival as a value. What is good for the species is what makes for its survival. What is good for the individual is what promotes his well-being. What is good for a culture is what permits it to solve its problems. There are, as we have seen, other kinds of values, but they eventually take second place to survival. (Skinner 1974:205)

It was presumably because of these evolutionary beliefs in the value of the survival of the species that Skinner believed passionately that Behaviourism should try to solve the problems of the world: 'The major problems facing the world today can be solved only if we improve our understanding of human behavior.'

(ibid.,8), and 'In the behavioristic view, man can now control his own destiny because he knows what must be done and how to do it' (251). One would have supposed that Behaviourism teaches the precise opposite. Having spent so much time showing that the individual is entirely passive to the environment, and denying the existence of purpose as a mentalistic illusion, it is therefore quite bizarre to find Skinner suddenly invoking these apparently discredited ideas in his proposals for controlling human destiny and saving the world. Indeed, he never faces up to the fundamental problem that if there is no such thing as the mind, and if consciousness and reason are illusions, how can Behaviourism itself, or the rest of science for that matter, claim to be objectively true?

His idea of society was also confused: on the one hand he held the naive materialist view that '[Behaviorism] reduces social processes to the behavior of individuals', (241), but, on the other hand, he had always maintained that these individuals cannot be autonomous. Who then is to control a society's (let alone the world's) development and apply proper Behaviourist remedies?

> The question represents the age-old mistake of looking to the individual rather than to the world in which he lives. It will not be a benevolent dictator, a compassionate therapist, a devoted teacher, or a public-spirited industrialist who will design a way of life in the interests of everyone. We must look instead at the conditions under which people govern, give help, teach, and arrange incentive systems in particular ways. In other words we must look to the culture as a social environment. (206)

Rather obviously however the 'culture as a social environment' could not begin to act in the purposeful and coherent manner required to impose Behaviourist theory as a way of life on any real group of people, and in the novel *Walden Two* (1962) where

Skinner fantasises about his own version of Utopia, he indeed falls back on the age-old tradition of the benevolent dictator. This turns out to be Skinner himself, thinly disguised as the psychologist Frazier, who has set up a successful colony run on Behaviourist principles and which is administered by a committee of self-appointed and self-perpetuating planners. Their aim is to condition the community members from birth to behave in the interests of the community (though he never explains how *they* have been conditioned to do this). Traditionally, as Frazier says, 'The behavior of the individual has been shaped according to revelations of "good conduct", never as the result of experimental study. But why not experiment? The questions are simple enough. What is the best behavior for the individual so far as the group is concerned? And how can the individual be induced to behave in that way? Why not explore these questions in a scientific spirit?' (1962:105)

One of Skinner's main targets is the family: 'The family is the frailest of modern institutions. Its weakness is evident to everyone' (137). It is 'an ancient form of community, and the customs and habits which have been set up to perpetuate it are out of place in a society which is not based on blood ties' (138). So while in Walden Two men and women are allowed to marry for personal gratification, their children are removed as babies and reared communally in growing pens by experts, because ordinary people do not have the intricate scientific skills to produce individuals with the requisite properties for the community. 'Home is not the place to raise children'(142)... The hereditary connection will be minimized to the point of being forgotten. Long before that, it will be possible to breed through artificial insemination without altering the personal relations between husband and wife' (144).

Not only must all competition within the community be removed, but drawing attention to exceptional achievement is undesirable because it points up the unexceptional achievement of others. 'Our decision to eliminate personal aggrandizement arose quite rationally from the fact that we are thinking about the whole group'(169). Personal friendship itself must also be eliminated as a threat to the group: '...no one in Walden Two ever acts for the benefit of anyone else except as the agent of the community. Personal favoritism [by which he means friendship], like personal gratitude, has been destroyed by our cultural engineers' (235).

At the end of the book, Frazier is looking forward to the kind of society that it will be possible to produce:

'What remains to be done?', [Frazier] said, his eyes flashing. 'Well, what do you say to the design of personalities? Would that interest you? The control of temperament? Give me the specifications, and I'll give you the man! What do you say to the control of motivation, building the interests which will make men most productive and most successful? Does that seem to you fantastic? Yet some of the techniques are available, and more can be worked out experimentally. Think of the possibilities! A society in which there is no failure, no boredom, no duplication of effort!

And what about the cultivation of special abilities? Do we know anything about the circumstances in the life of the child which give him a mathematical mind? Or make him musical? Almost nothing at all! These things are left to accident or blamed on heredity...But we've got to make a start. There's no virtue in accident. Let us control the lives of our children and see what we can make of them.'

Frazier began to pace back and forth, his hands still thrust in his pockets.

'My hunch is – and when I feel this way about a hunch, it's never wrong – that we shall eventually find out, not only what makes a child mathematical, but how to make better mathematicians! If we can't solve a problem, we can create men who can! And better artists! And better craftsmen!... And all the while we shall be improving upon our social and cultural design. We know almost nothing about the special capacities of the *group*...

The problem of efficient group structure alone is enough to absorb anyone's interest. An organisation of a committee of scientists or a panel of script writers is far from what it could be. But we lack control in the world at large to investigate more efficient structures. Here , on the contrary – here we can begin to understand and build the Superorganism. We can construct groups of artists and scientists who will act as smoothly and efficiently as champion football teams.

And all the while, Burris, we shall be increasing the net power of the community by leaps and bounds. Does it seem to you unreasonable to estimate that the present efficiency of society is of the order of a fraction of one per cent? *A fraction of one per cent!* And you ask what remains to be done!' (292-93)

Although many readers may think that Skinner was as mad as a hatter, his materialism is main-stream, and although Behaviourism itself is now dead, having been fundamentally discredited in particular by Chomsky's revolutionary innovations in linguistics, and by developments in computer science[18], his ideal community of Walden Two nevertheless has many ideas in common with those other totalitarian Utopias that were constructed in the twentieth century. These are: central planning by unelected scientific experts, the need for harmony, uniformity, efficiency, and the removal of all painful experience, the abolition of the family and its replacement by the communal education of children and eugenic breeding, compulsory altruism and the abolition of class differences (except those between the planners and the planned-for), the elimination of competition and all private relationships, and individuals generally moulded by social engineering to be compliant and happy. The colony,

Walden Two, is everything, while the individual members have no more importance than laboratory rats. We can take up these themes in the next section.

3. Collectivism and its terrors

Modern industrial society presents a whole range of moral problems, as did those of the ancient civilisations, that are associated with complexity and the breakdown of rules and standards and meaning, conflicts of values, and the erosion of the sense of belonging that had existed in the simpler societies of hunter-gatherers and farmers, and which nowadays can only be faintly recaptured in rural villages. In the small, traditional, communal societies studied by anthropologists people have simple and direct face-to-face relations with each other, which are predominantly based on family and kinship and regulated by custom. Material needs are basic, everyone produces what they need for themselves, there is no exploitation, and class conflict does not exist. By the nineteenth century, however, Western industrial societies, governed by the state, were vastly bigger and interactions were mainly between strangers, organised on the basis of functional efficiency and other economic and political considerations by government bureaucracies and large industrial organisations. Human relations had become far more impersonal and indirect, based on a monetary economy, rational self-interest and economic calculation which weakened the customary bonds of family, kinship, and religion, while economic exploitation and class antagonism were basic features of capitalist society.

Many thinkers in the nineteenth century were repelled by these class divisions, the greed and selfishness engendered by capitalism, and the exploitation and squalor of the workers produced by industrialism. It is important to realise that altruistic reverence for the values of community and self-sacrifice in its defence, and the rejection of individualism as *selfishness*, have been essential moral foundations of modern totalitarianism. The communal life of the early Christians, as described in the New Testament, was thoroughly familiar to Western society, but Engels, like many others who wished for the root-and-branch reform of society invoked the old ideal of the Noble Savage, specifically the way of life of the North American Indians. As described by the pioneering anthropologist Lewis Henry Morgan (*Ancient Society* 1877) these were believed to embody the ideals of liberty, equality, and fraternity, where property was held in common, women were free, and disputes were settled by the community. Engels quotes Morgan:

> All the members of an Iroquois *gens* [clan] were personally free, and they were bound to defend each other's freedom; they were equal in privileges and personal rights, the sachems and chiefs claiming no superiority, and they were a brotherhood bound together by ties of kin. Liberty, equality and fraternity, though never formulated, were cardinal principles of the gens. (53)
>
> There cannot be any poor and destitute – the communistic households and the *gentes* know their duties toward the aged, sick and disabled. All are free and equal – the women included. There is no room yet for slaves, nor for the subjugation of foreign tribes.[19]

The question was therefore how to return us to the communal society of early Man, but at the same time retain the benefits of modern technology and industrialism without the squalor, without the class divisions which capitalism had done so much to exacerbate, and without the personal alienation created by industrial production and mass urban society. This was often represented as building the Kingdom of Heaven on earth, and by some this was taken quite literally. Christians have always been major critics of capitalist, industrial society and of the exploitation and class-conflict that it has produced, so the idea of Christian Socialism has been a powerful force in politics. But the dangers of forgetting that 'My Kingdom is not of this world', and the requirement to love God as well as our neighbour, are well illustrated by the eccentric French nobleman Saint-Simon who held that science and technology had made the traditional Christianity of prayer, church-going, liturgy, and individual spiritual life completely obsolete mumbo-jumbo. The only principle of Christianity henceforth is that:

> Men should treat each other as brothers. This sublime principle comprises *all that is divine in the Christian religion...* [my italics] (Markham 1952:83). Doubtless all Christians desire eternal life, but the only way of obtaining it consists in working during this life for the welfare of the human race. (101) ...New Christianity is called upon to pronounce anathema upon theology, and to condemn as unholy any doctrine trying to teach men that there is any other way of obtaining eternal life, except that of working with all their might for the improvement of the conditions of life of their fellow men (105).

The New Christian, then, obtains salvation not by prayer and closeness to God but by building a gas-works to provide cheap lighting for the working-class. This led directly to the Social Gospel movement in the United States:

> They argued from pulpits and political gatherings and in the intellectual press for a total and complete reconception of scripture in which redemption could only be achieved collectively. Conservative theologians argued that only the individual could be born again. The progressive Christians claimed that individuals no longer mattered and that only the state could serve as divine intercessor. The Baptist Social Gospel preacher argued that the state must become 'the

medium through which the people shall co-operate in their search for the kingdom of God and its righteousness' (Goldberg 2007: 217).

Inevitably, the logical conclusion of this exclusive focus on material progress was the disappearance of genuinely spiritual religion altogether. In 1965 the Baptist minister Harvey Cox wrote *The Secular City*,

> ...and argued for a kind of desacralisation of Christianity in favour of a new transcendence found in the technopolis, which was 'the place of human control, of rational planning, of bureaucratic organization'. Modern religion and spirituality required 'the breaking of all supernatural myths and sacred symbols'. Instead we must spiritualize the material culture to perfect man and society through technology and social planning... Authentic worship was done not by kneeling in a church but by 'standing in a picket line' (236).

This 'desacralised' Christianity has rather obviously ceased to be Christianity at all; it has morphed into a purely secular utilitarianism, but to attain its social ends those communitarian values to which I referred earlier are not enough. They need the political power of the centralised state to provide that rational planning by which the resources of science, technology, and industry can be harnessed to master nature for the material good of the people. Such a project inevitably tends to acquire those features of Walden Two that we have already encountered: a rational, scientific plan devised by unelected experts in the psychological and social sciences. And because such a plan must be true, almost by definition, omnipotent rulers are justified in using the centralised political power of the state and all the forces of education to create a 'New Man': to suppress competition, individualism, and the family, and enforce uniformity, altruism, and community spirit, and direct the forces of modern industry and technology to the common good of progress towards Utopia. Anyone who resists this benevolent scheme is, again almost by definition, an enemy of the people and can be dealt with as such. In the twentieth century we came to know this as fascism, whose basic characteristics have been shared by totalitarian regimes of both 'Right' and 'Left':

> Fascism is a religion of the state. It assumes the organic unity of the body politic and longs for a national leader attuned to the will of the people. It is totalitarian in that it views everything as political and holds that any action by the state is justified to achieve the common good. It takes responsibility for all aspects of life, including our health and well-being, and seeks to impose uniformity of thought and action, whether by force or through regulation and social pressure. Everything, including the economy and religion, must be aligned with its objectives. Any rival identity is part of the 'problem' and therefore defined as the enemy (Goldberg 2007: 23).

In the background of this whole enterprise is the inherent worship of power, as the necessary means of bringing the New World into being, and we shall see that power and the extermination of opponents of the new order has a peculiar fascination for intellectuals. The opportunities of political power in fascist states also have a special appeal to narcissists, and in the form of 'the cult of personality' they seem to be almost inevitable features of totalitarian dictators whose monstrous egotism reaches its supreme manifestation in the person of Adolf Hitler.

4. Communism

So the belief in a primitive communism of Noble Savages where liberty, equality, and fraternity reigned, goods were held in common, and women were not yet subjugated by the tyranny of patriarchal marriage, was a central foundation myth of many utopian schemes from the Enlightenment onwards. Marxism, the most notable of these schemes, was presented as a rigorous materialistic science of human society, achieving for our understanding of social evolution what Darwin had achieved for biological evolution. The mode of production determined the social structure which, after the rise of private property had destroyed the first primitive society, had been dominated by a series of class struggles. The inexorable logic of dialectical materialism leads us through the stages of slavery and feudalism to the final conflict, that between the bourgeoisie and the workers, whose revolutionary overthrow of capitalism will lead to communism. The inevitable processes of social evolution therefore produce a return to the original communism, but this time on the basis of advanced technology, with material abundance for all.

The historical process must inevitably be violent because it consists of the successive rise and overthrow of ruling classes until the final destruction of the bourgeoisie by the proletariat that will usher in communism. This class struggle can no more be peaceful than the struggle for survival in nature and according to Marxists, critics of the elimination of the bourgeoisie for social evolutionary reasons fail to remember the cost in death and suffering caused by biological evolution.

In Marxist theory there is no basic human nature since the individual's consciousness is moulded by his society: 'Does it require deep intuition to comprehend that man's ideas, views and conceptions, in one word, man's consciousness, changes with every change in the conditions of his material existence, in his social relations and in his social life?'[20] Individuals are therefore a kind of raw material which only acquires value when processed by the right kind of society. There will be one type of ethics among hunter-gatherers where liberty, equality, and fraternity are the norm, another militaristic ethic in feudal societies, and another capitalist ethic in bourgeois society, where selfishness and greed are the norm, as is so well demonstrated in the beliefs of Objectivism. In the future, again, Communist Man will have gone beyond the selfishness of bourgeois Man and will have been conditioned to work altruistically and happily for the common good.

Liberty, equality, and fraternity were therefore good because they were the product of a co-operative (=good) *social organisation*, not because these were individual virtues, still less because they were individual human rights. Marx and Engels had no time for human rights, least of all the natural right to own property which they believed legitimated bourgeois egotism and selfishness. Since morality was the product of a particular economic system, bourgeois morality was bound to be different from communist morality. This assumption that class was the basis of all intellectual and moral life inevitably led to a relativistic conception of all standards of ethics, justice, and truth, even scientific truth, as when Mendelian genetics was dismissed as bourgeois science and replaced by Lysenkoism. But as the philosopher Bernard Williams has remarked, all relativistic theories need a non-relativistic justification, and the Communists had an urgent political need to claim that Marxism was nevertheless an objectively true theory of history because this was the basis of their legitimacy.

Despite their ideal vision of communism as a society of freedom and equality where the state would wither away, everyone knows that Marx and Engels had actually supplied an ideology of class conflict and historically inevitable revolution that provided an excellent foundation for a totalitarian state ruled by scientific experts. But they never worked out the political process by which, after the violent overthrow of capitalism, the communist society could actually be achieved. This was the contribution of Lenin who believed that the workers did not have the necessary political consciousness for revolution, and that left to themselves they would be content with trades union activities. Historical forces alone were not enough, then, to produce communism, and revolutionary consciousness had to be brought to the workers by an intellectual elite with a thorough grasp of Marxist theory, who were ruthless, highly disciplined professional activists and in the form of the Communist Party would act as the vanguard of the proletariat.

After the Revolution, the Party under Lenin and Stalin allowed no deviation from its policies, and this highly authoritarian regime was officially justified by the scientific status of Marxism. As one leading Party member said to Isaiah Berlin,

> We are a scientifically governed society, ...and if there is no room for free thinking in physics – a man who questions the laws of motion is obviously ignorant or mad – why should we, Marxists, who have discovered the laws of history and society, permit free thinking in the social sphere? Freedom to be wrong is not freedom; you seem to think that we lack freedom of political discussion; I simply do not understand what you mean. Truth liberates: we are freer than you in the West.[21]

It was also admitted that this dictatorship was a necessary stage in the ultimate achievement of Communism:

> The experience of public organisations in the socialist countries has already demonstrated that the most effective means of combating selfish individualism, which is the chief enemy of communist ethics, is to counter it by active collectivism. Collectivism most of all corresponds to the ideal of communism because it regards service for the common good as the highest standard of behaviour. At the same time it most of all corresponds to the interests of the individual personality, fostering in it the most lofty human traits... There can be no doubt that it is in the collective that the man of the future

is moulded, the man for whom the principles of communism will become the foundation of his consciousness, the voice of his conscience.[22]

At the present time, while society is being transformed, this collectivism has to be compulsory, using the full coercive power of the state. Only in a future purely communist society will 'the grounds for any measures of coercion disappear. The relations of domination and subordination are finally replaced by free co-operation. There is no need for the state. The need for legal regimentation withers away'.[23] While awaiting this happy outcome terror could therefore be used without compunction, and Stalin, for example, when making out his lists of those to be executed made a point of including people whom he knew to be innocent because 'If the innocent know they are safe from execution they will not fear us'.

Marxist ethics were strongly utilitarian and argued that it was morally justifiable to kill hundreds of class enemies now if thousands will enjoy the fruits of communism in the future. The obligation to work toward the overthrow of the bourgeoisie may very well include the duty to kill, and to do so in very large numbers. Kruschev explains: 'Our cause is sacred. He whose hand will tremble, who will stop midway, whose knees will shake before he destroys tens and hundreds of enemies, he will lead the revolution into danger. Whoever will spare a few lives of enemies, will pay for it with hundreds and thousands of lives of the better sons of our fathers'.[24] Indeed, Mao Tse Tung was quite willing to contemplate the sacrifice of half the Chinese population in a nuclear war if this could bring about world communism, and it has been estimated that he actually caused the deaths of around 45-55 million of his own people during the Great Leap Forward.[25] This indifference to the value of individual life seems quite characteristic of Marxist intellectuals. The late Tony Benn described Chairman Mao as 'The greatest man of the twentieth century'[26], and in a BBC television interview with Canadian author and politician Michael Ignatieff, the greatly admired Marxist historian Eric Hobsbawm, when asked if 20 million deaths would have been justified if the communist utopia had been achieved, agreed that this would have been the case.[27]

In Marxism we therefore find the same indifference to the value of the individual as in Walden Two and as we shall find in Nazism, and the same emphasis on competition and conflict as the driving force of the evolutionary process as in Darwinism, but in this case the competitors are not different races or nations, but different economic classes. It was presumably because Marx saw the human race as divided into different classes, rather than societies or ethnic groups, that he could be universalistic: 'workers of the world unite – you have nothing to lose but your chains'.

But the next section explores an additional twist to collectivism, the belief in radical, biologically based inequalities in Man, both racial and individual, and the kind of moral order it can produce.

5. Nazism

It tends to be forgotten that the Nazis were National *Socialists*, and had rather similar ideas to Marx and Engels about the value of community, and the need for individual self-sacrifice and the abolition of traditional class distinctions:

> The seduction of Nazism was its appeal to community, its attempt to restore via an all-powerful state a sense of belonging to those lost in modern society. Modernization, industrialization, and secularization sowed doubt and alienation among the masses. The Nazis promised to make people belong to something larger than themselves. The spirit of 'all for one, one for all' suffused every Nazi pageant and parade.[28]

After coming to power as Chancellor in 1933, Hitler's Nazi regime was certainly socialist, bringing employers and labour under the control of the state, dedicated to full employment, spending on public works, and raising the standard of living for the workers. The Nazis also expended a great deal of effort in socialising the people and breaking down class distinctions, organising everyone from the cradle to the grave in a collective way of life – such as the Hitler Youth, the German Women's League, and sports and leisure activities like Strength Through Joy.

To this extent Hitler's regime can be described as 'fascist', but the underlying reality was very different and the Nazis strongly objected to being called fascists. Fascist dictators gained their power from being at the head of the all-powerful state but Hitler's aim, on the contrary, was absolute power based on his own unique status as the *Führer* (leader) of the German people. While Lenin, Stalin, Mao, and other Communist dictators seem to have believed that they were legitimated by the Marxist cause, Hitler's only cause was himself and his own power. The Third Reich therefore derived its authority from the all-powerful *Führer*, and Hitler:

...deliberately destroyed the state's ability to function in favour of his personal omnipotence and irreplaceability, and ...he did so right from the start. A state's ability to function is based upon its constitution, whether written or unwritten. The Third Reich, however, had neither had a written nor an unwritten constitution from (at the latest) the autumn of 1934. It neither recognized nor respected any specific rights restricting the power of the state *vis-a-vis* the citizen, nor did it possess even the indispensable minimum of a constitution, i.e. procedural rules for the state that would define the rights of the various state authorities with regard to each other and ensure that their activities were meaningfully integrated. Hitler, on the contrary, had deliberately brought about a state of affairs in which the most various autonomous authorities were ranged alongside and against one another, without defined boundaries, in competition, and overlapping – and only he was at the head of all of them. Only thus was he able to secure for himself the completely unrestricted freedom of action which he intended to have in all directions (Haffner 2003: 43) ...Hitler was not interested in the state... He was concerned only with nations and races, not with states. The state to him was "only a means to an end", the end, in brief, being the waging of war (86).

Hitler was an extreme example of the narcissistic personality: always exceptionally conceited and with a grievance against the world, he regarded himself as an artist and architect of genius; he was completely incapable of self-criticism and became enraged by even the most trivial criticisms from others; he was also entirely humourless except when laughing at other people's misfortunes or weaknesses; while he could be charming he had no capacity for friendship, and could not tolerate anyone with superior abilities. He therefore preferred to surround himself with subordinates and nonentities whom he enjoyed humiliating and subjecting to endless monologues. 'The most basic single characteristic of both his personal life and his system of government can be reduced to one overriding need: to force others to do his will'.[29]

But while he was deluded about his artistic status, he had an extraordinary personal magnetism, particularly based on the power of his eyes; he had an astonishing memory, which he used to browbeat his subordinates into submission; he was a demagogic orator of tremendous power; and he was a master of propaganda, terror, and political strategy, with an unerring instinct for weakness in his opponents. He had, of course, the utmost contempt for democracy and regarded the people, like women, as fit only to be dominated and manipulated: 'Hitler considered mankind treacherous, irrational, base, and generally incapable of judgment. The people were 'as stupid as they are forgetful'; they were 'weak and bestial' or 'lazy and cowardly'. He spoke of the 'granite-like stupidity of humanity' and 'the great stupid mutton-herd of our sheep-like people'.[30]

From his accession to power in 1933, Hitler transformed the whole fortunes of the German people, and by 1940, with the defeat of France and the British withdrawal from the continent, Hitler had made them the masters of Europe. And he had ensured that he was not simply the leader of a state, like Mussolini, but had become the personification of the German people, the *Volksgeist*: 'He is the incarnation of the Spirit of the People, and it is only through his interpretation that the people is led to a full realization of itself.' This was legal reality: 'Our constitution is the will of the Fuhrer'.[31] As Hitler said of himself: "*Ich bin das deutsche Volk!*"[32] Has there ever been, in any society, a greeting like 'Heil Hitler!', or a society in which millions could say 'Adolf Hitler is my conscience'?

As Führer of the Germans, Adolf Hitler probably exerted more direct personal power than any ruler in history. He created both his own political theory and a government that could not exist without him. It was he who set the standards for art, music, medicine, and poetry. His whim became national law. He dictated statutes which set forth the religion of household servants, the colors artists could use in paintings, the way lobsters were to be cooked in restaurants, and how physics would be taught in the universities...[33]

The German people were therefore his to use as he pleased, and the use that he had for them was war. For Hitler, warfare between different peoples, in the struggle for survival and living space (*Lebensraum*), was the natural condition of mankind: 'Every being strives for expansion and every nation strives for world domination'[34], but even here, it was not the occupation of territory that really attracted Hitler, but the possibilities of extermination on a vast scale. (In his drive for *Lebensraum* in the East, he certainly contemplated the murder of thirty million Slavs.) Here we have to understand that Hitler derived a deep satisfaction from the contemplation of human slaughter.

> Throughout the war Hitler continually gave evidence of this lust for blood, this physical delight in the intellectual contemplation of slaughter for its own sake. The generals, hardened automata, notorious as impersonal men of blood and iron, were shocked at such positive emotions, and have given numerous instances of it. During the Polish campaign, Halder maintained that the storming of Warsaw was unnecessary; it would fall of itself, since the Polish Army no longer existed; but Hitler insisted that Warsaw must be destroyed. His artist's temper aroused, he described the delicious scenes which he demanded – the sky darkened, a million tons of shells raining down on the city, and the people drowned in blood; 'then his eyes popped out of his head, and he became quite a different person. He was suddenly seized by a lust for blood'. (Trevor-Roper 1952: 78-9)

Hitler's slaughters were often militarily senseless, and even counterproductive, as in the use of mass transport facilities for conveying the Jews to the camps in 1944, and in the Soviet Union, where the Germans were initially welcomed as liberators. 'Hitler's mass murders were committed during the war, but they were not acts of war. On the contrary, it may be said that he used the war as a pretext for committing mass murders which had nothing to do with the war, but for which he had always felt a personal need.'[35]

He was not, therefore, a patriot who sacrificed himself to the service of the German people but who sacrificed *them* to his service instead: 'I shall become the greatest man in history. I have to gain immortality even if the whole German people perishes in the process'.[36]

Did he love the Germans? He had chosen Germany without knowing Germany. Strictly speaking he never came to know it. The Germans were his chosen people because his inborn power instinct pointed to them like a compass needle as to the greatest power potential in Europe in his day. And it was only as an instrument of power that he was ever genuinely interested in them (Haffner 2003:164).

Indeed, once it became clear that Germany was going to lose the war, Hitler did his best to ensure that the Germans perished with him. 'On this point, too, I am icily cold. If one day the German nation is no longer sufficiently strong or sufficiently ready for sacrifice to stake its blood for its existence, then let it perish and be annihilated by some stronger power...'[37] In late 1944, after the Allied invasion,

...he ordered any German who uttered the obvious and current thought that the war was lost *and who hinted that he wished to survive it* [my italics] to be mercilessly hanged or beheaded. Hitler had always been a great hater and derived much inward pleasure from killing. The force of Hitler's hatred, the homicidal drive in Hitler which had raged for years against Jews, Poles and Russians, was now quite openly turning against Germans (Haffner 2003: 154).

On 7th September, 1944, in the face of the Allied advance, he decreed, 'Not a German stock of wheat is to feed the enemy, not a German mouth to give him information, not a German hand to offer him help. He is to find... nothing but death, annihilation, and hatred', and ordered the whole population in the West to abandon their homes, on foot if necessary, rather than surrender to the Allies. He ordered the complete destruction of all German industry, transport, communications, and supplies, and on 20 April, 1945, he 'called forth an orgy of destruction. Farms and woodlands were to be burned, cattle slaughtered. Works of art, monuments, palaces, castles, churches, theatres – all were to be obliterated'.[38]

Communists could at least claim that Marxism was an intellectually serious theory of society and history, even though it turned out to be disastrously wrong, but this could not be said of Nazism which was a strange concoction of pseudo-scientific and pseudo-religious propaganda designed to justify the claims of the Führer to absolute power, with the Nazi Party as his instrument. While Stalin was unambiguously an atheist, Hitler's religious beliefs are more obscure because they are wrapped up in Nazi propaganda. He had to get elected by the German people, and to have declared himself an atheist would have been politically impossible in the German culture of the times, particularly because of atheism's close association with Communism. He often referred to himself as specially chosen by the Almighty, (or by destiny, or by the goddess Fate), and compared himself to Jesus, the Messiah with a divine mission to save Germany and the world from the plague of international Jewry. Nazi propaganda often referred to 'holy crusades', 'sacred oaths', and 'religious duty', but these were nothing more than familiar cultural motifs used to enhance the Nazi image.

This image seems to have depended rather more on the Wagnerian world of the pagan Germanic gods, especially Wotan, the Wild Huntsman with a trail of desolation and corpses behind him. Nazi pageants and parades had a strongly pagan aspect, and the revival of what was thought to be the ancient Aryan culture of the Germanic Volk was a very important aspect of Nazi propaganda, particularly by Himmler and the SS, with their fantastic notions of race.

Outside its propaganda value, however, the only thing Hitler admired about Christianity was its intolerance:

The greatness of every mighty organization embodying an idea in this world lies in the religious fanaticism and intolerance with which, fanatically convinced of its own right, it intolerantly imposes its will against all others... The greatness of Christianity did not lie in attempted negotiations for compromise with any similar philosophical opinions in the ancient world, but in its inexorable fanaticism in preaching and fighting for its own doctrine (*Mein Kampf*, 318).

But he had complete contempt for its teachings:

In Hitler's eyes Christianity was a religion fit only for slaves; he detested its ethics in particular. Its teaching, he declared, was a rebellion against the natural law of selection by struggle and the survival of the fittest. 'Taken to its logical extreme, Christianity would mean the systematic cultivation of the human failure.' ...once the war was over, he promised himself, he would root out and destroy the influence of the Christian Churches (Bullock 1962:389).

Hitler's basic beliefs were fundamentally biological, obsessed with race, blood, bodily health and purity, disease (especially syphilis), and the necessity for eternal war and the survival of the fittest. Here, Darwin's theory of evolution provided a very powerful and supportive world-view, whose political implications when applied to Man were obvious to everybody. This is why T.H.Huxley referred to it as 'the gladiatorial theory of existence' that should be rigorously excluded from human society. In *The Descent of Man* (1871), Darwin had made it absolutely clear that incessant tribal warfare, in particular, had been essential for developing the co-operative human qualities of loyalty, sympathy, and self-sacrifice: 'A tribe rich in the above qualities would spread and be victorious over other tribes: but in the course of time it would, judging from all past history, be in its turn overcome by some other tribe still more highly endowed. Thus the social and moral qualities would tend slowly to advance and be diffused throughout the world.'[39]

While modern hunter-gatherers certainly fight, and in the course of a man's lifetime he can have a high probability of dying a violent death, the group exterminations envisaged by Darwin in fact seem very rare. It is also striking that Darwin here places so much emphasis on violent competition, since in fact Darwinian competition only requires one group to *out-reproduce* another, not actually to kill them. So, one group that co-operates more effectively in hunting than another group will out-reproduce it without any need for violence. While warfare has undoubtedly been a major factor in social evolution Darwin's exclusive emphasis on violence here is distinctly one-sided.

Darwin also maintained the same exaggerated picture of relentless cruelty and violence in relation to the treatment of the sick among primitive peoples:

With savages, the weak in body and mind are soon eliminated; and those that survive commonly exhibit a vigorous state of health. We civilised men, on the other hand, do our utmost to check the process of elimination: we build asylums for the imbecile, the maimed, and the sick; we institute poor laws; and our medical men exert their utmost skill to save the life of everyone to the last moment... Thus the weak members of civilised societies propagate their kind.[40]

While Darwin was a kind man, who would have been horrified by the Nazis, there is no doubt that his powerful general picture of natural selection in many minds seemed to legitimate violent competition in which the weak were trampled underfoot as a law of Nature.[41]

Darwin's work was especially influential in German scientific circles, and was quickly applied to contemporary politics and economics, where its relevance to competition and warfare was perfectly obvious. Cases in point were Bismarck's successful wars against Austria, Denmark, and France and his forcible unification of all the states of Germany under Prussian rule in a new Empire in 1870. As early as 1863 Professor Ernst Haeckel, Darwin's most important scientific advocate in Germany, said 'For it is the same principles, the struggle for existence and natural selection, working in civil society, which drive the peoples irresistibly onwards, step by step, to higher cultural stages... This progress is a natural law which no human law can permanently suppress.'[42]

Darwinian ideas increasingly influenced social thinking as the century progressed. For example, an important Social Darwinist in the 1890s who argued for the benefits of both individual and collective competition was Otto Ammon: 'In its full effect war is a blessing for humanity, since it offers the only means to measure the strengths of one nation to another and to grant the victory to the fittest. War is the highest and most majestic form of the struggle for existence and cannot be disposed of and therefore also cannot be abolished.'[43]

Gumplowicz, an Austrian professor of sociology, maintained in his book *The Racial Struggle* that:

War is inevitable and peace is merely an armistice in the continuous battle among races and groups for survival. He denied that Europeans could come to a peaceful settlement with Asians and Africans. Rather, the weaker would be eliminated. He also justified the subjugation of one ethnic group by another, asserting that this is the foundation of civilization and that 'we do not hesitate to recognize that the most cruel and barbarous conquerors are the blind instruments of human progress and powerfully promote civilization, nay even found it.'[44]

Many other contemporary thinkers could be cited to show that Darwinian ideas were a fashionable part of the intellectual culture not only of the English-speaking world but especially of Germany before World War I. Hitler most probably had never read any of Darwin's original works, but he would not have needed to because the basic theory of natural selection as applied to nations and human competition was simple and straight-forward, and had been so widely popularised. It is worth noting that at this time 'Germany was a land of high general culture, with the largest reading public of any country in the world. In the lower middle class, there was a tremendous educational urge. People who in other countries would read light novels and popular magazines devoured works on art, science, history, and above all philosophy.'[45]

So while it would be absurd to claim that Darwinian theory *caused* German militarism, or Hitler's ambitions for conquest, it is obvious from *Mein Kampf* and from his *Tabletalk* that he was thoroughly imbued with the beliefs that war and the elimination of the weak and inferior by the strong were Nature's means of ensuring progress, and also that complete individual submission to the group was necessary to this end.

In the struggle for daily bread all those who are weak and sickly or less determined succumb, while the struggle of the males for the female grants the right or opportunity to propagate only to the healthiest. And struggle is always a means for improving a species' health and power of resistance and, therefore, a cause of its higher development. If the process were different, all further and higher development would cease and the opposite would occur. For, since the inferior always predominates numerically over the best, if both had the same possibility of preserving life and propa-gating, the inferior would multiply so much more rapidly that in the end the best would inevitably be driven into the background, unless a correction of this state of affairs were undertaken (*Mein Kampf*, 259).

This process of struggle requires the utmost self-sacrifice and loyalty to the group:

> The greater the readiness to subordinate purely personal interests, the higher rises the ability to establish [cohesive] communities. This self-sacrificing will to give one's personal labour and if necessary one's own life for others is most strongly developed in the Aryan. The Aryan is not greatest in his mental qualities as such, but in the extent of his willingness to put all his abilities in the service of the community. In him the instinct of self-preservation has reached the noblest form, since he willingly subordinates his own ego to the life of the community and, if the hour demands it, even sacrifices it (*Mein Kampf*, 270).

Eugenics, both by selective breeding and the elimination of the sick, is also an intrinsic component of the Darwinian view of Man as animal. Eugenics was widely accepted by scientists and social theorists in the United States and Britain, as well as in Germany, and Hitler, following this principle, began the extermination of the mentally and physically handicapped soon after gaining power. As Nietzsche rather pithily expressed it: 'The sick are the greatest danger for the well. The weaker, not the stronger, are the strong's undoing... Those born wrong, the miscarried, the broken – they it is, the *weakest*, who are undermining the vitality of the race, poisoning our trust in life, and putting humanity in question.'[46]

The mention of Nietzsche brings us to another powerful component of Nazism, its obsession with his idea of the Superman, who had the inherent right to dominate and exploit the masses. Interestingly, Darwin also had a very important influence on Nietzsche (1844-1900), and through his philosophy, on Hitler. In Nietzsche's view, Darwin had shown that both animals and Man had evolved purely fortuitously by variation and selection, without any guiding purpose: God was therefore dead and life and the universe had no meaning. While some felt liberated by Darwinism, Nietzsche thought it was a disaster and that we needed a fresh morality rooted in the new world revealed by science, which restored the special place of Man in the scheme of things but on a naturalistic basis. He had, however, the utmost contempt for atheists who deluded themselves that their morality of liberty, equality, and fraternity could survive undisturbed by the disappearance of God, and would have made mincemeat out of Grayling and Kurtz and the rest of the Humanists.

From his classical studies he believed that the Greeks of the sixth century BC had been driven by competition and the need to win. In this process, the superior defeat the inferior, and slavery in Nietzsche's view was right and natural, and the basis of Greek achievements. 'The Greeks were cruel, savage, and predatory; yet they had become the most humane people of antiquity, the inventors of philosophy, science and tragedy, the first and finest European nation'.[47] He was particularly impressed by Heraclitus and his belief that war is the father of all things, or as Nietzsche put it, that 'strife is the perpetual food of the soul'. Ordinary morality is essentially custom, which enforces conformity to each society's particular norms, but great men overturn the conventional and the customary; in one sense, this is 'evil', but in a higher sense it is good because it leads to the highest triumphs of civilisation:

The strongest and most evil spirits have hitherto advanced mankind the most... they have again and again reawoken the sense of comparison, of contradiction, of delight in the new, the hazardous, the untried; they have compelled mankind to set opinion against opinion, ideal against ideal. Generally it has been by force of arms, by overturning boundary-stones, by violating piety: but also through new religions and moralities!... the evil impulses are just as useful, indispensable and preservative of the species as the good: only their function is different.[48]

The basic idea underlying Nietzsche's philosophy is therefore 'the Will to Power', shared by Man with the animals, but which uniquely in Man included the ability to master the self. Nietzsche was now able to treat the Darwinian struggle for existence as included in the Will to Power. His friendship with Wagner was also of fundamental importance here: '...the decisive insight from which the theory of the will to power grew came when he recognized that Wagner's tremendous art-works were essentially a product of his equally tremendous need to dominate other people.'[49] The Will to Power therefore included the whole range of human achievement, from philosophical debate, to art, to lawgiving, to the conquest of one people by another. Even love derives from the desire to exert power over the loved one, while asceticism is the desire to master ourselves, the mark of the highest form of Man – the *Übermensch* or Superman. Man is again raised above the animals, but this time on a naturalistic basis:

All creatures desire power but only man is able to desire power over himself; only man has the requisite amount of power to achieve *self*-mastery. The distinction between man and animal, obliterated by Darwin, is restored – and without recourse to the supernatural; moral values, deprived of divine sanction, now receive a new, naturalistic sanction: quanta of power; human psychology is now understood in terms of power; 'good' is now understood as sublimated 'evil', the evil and the good passions being essentially the same, i.e. will to power.[50]

As Nietzsche expressed it,

What is good? Everything that heightens the feeling of power in man, the will to power, power itself.

What is bad? Everything that is born of weakness.

What is happiness? The feeling that power is *growing*, that resistance is overcome.

Not contentedness but more power; not peace but war; not virtue but fitness...

The weak and the failures shall perish: first principle of *our* love of man. And they shall even be given every possible assistance.

What is more harmful than any vice? Active pity for all the failures and all the weak: Christianity.
(Nietzsche, *The Antichrist*, §2)

The goal of mankind should therefore be to produce Supermen, genuinely higher beings and God's successors. There will then be two social moralities, the morality of the ruler, a noble morality, and a slave morality. The noble morality is that of conquerors and those who command: 'The noble man honours in himself the man of power, and also the man who has power over himself, who understands how to speak and how to keep silent, who enjoys practising severity and harshness upon himself and feels reverence for all that is severe and harsh...'[51]

The slave morality, as we might expect, is very different:

Suppose the abused, oppressed, suffering, unfree, those uncertain of themselves and the weary should moralise: what would their moral evaluations have in common? ...[T]hose qualities which serve to lighten the existence of suffering will be brought into prominence and flooded with light: here it is that sympathy, the kind and helping hand, the warm heart, patience, diligence, humility, friendliness, come into honour – for here these are the most useful qualities and virtually the only means of enduring the burden of existence.[52]

In Nietzsche's view these Christian and humane qualities are therefore despicable; they are not the expression of universal love at all but motivated by the fear, hatred, and envy that the inferior feel for their betters, the typical values of slaves. Hence his passionate loathing of Christianity: 'I call Christianity the one great curse, the one innermost perversion... One does well to put on gloves when reading the New Testament – the proximity of so much filth almost forces one to do this.'[53] While the Superman may be an artistic genius, like Wagner, he can equally be a conqueror like Napoleon or Alexander or one of a conquering class:

> One cannot fail to see at the core of all these noble races the animal of prey, the splendid *blonde beast* prowling about avidly in search of spoil and victory; this hidden core needs to erupt from time to time, the animal has to get out again and go back to the wilderness: the Roman, Arabian, Germanic, Japanese nobility, the Homeric heroes, the Scandinavian Vikings – they all shared this need. It is the noble races that have left behind them the concept 'barbarian' wherever they have gone.[54]

Nietzsche regarded these eruptions of barbarian vigour and domination as the origin of the state through conquest:

> ...the oldest 'state' ...appeared as a fearful tyranny and went on working until this raw material of people and semi-animals was... *moulded.* I employed the word 'state': it is self-evident what is meant – some herd of blonde beasts of prey, a conqueror and master race which, organised for war and the ability to organise, unhesitatingly lays its terrible claws upon a population perhaps tremendously superior in numbers but still formless and nomad. That is how the 'state' began on earth.[55]

Once the state is established it has no obligations to its subjects: the people are simply there to serve the interests of their superiors, the aristocratic class of Supermen whose transcendent excellence alone justifies the very existence of the people:

> The essential thing in a good and healthy aristocracy is... that it does *not* feel itself to be a function (of a kingdom or of a commonwealth), but as the *meaning* and highest justification thereof – that it should therefore accept with a good conscience the sacrifice of innumerable men who, *for its sake*, have to be suppressed and reduced to imperfect men, to slaves and tools. Its basic faith must be that society should *not* exist for the sake of society, but only as foundation and scaffolding upon which a select order of beings may raise itself to... a higher *existence*.[56]

It is true that Nietzsche thought more in terms of a *class* of Supermen rather than an actual *race*, had no interest in the idea of racial purity, and admired the Jews and the Poles while writing contemptuously of the Germans, so in these respects he would not have approved of Hitler's policies. But, these qualifications apart, it is rather obvious why his general philosophy should have been enthusiastically taken up by the Nazis, and how its specific teachings about the Superman and the masses combined very well with their generally Darwinian view of society:

> All values must be 'transvalued' accordingly: in place of equality, the recognition of innate superiority; in place of democracy, the aristocracy of the virile and the strong; in place of Christian humility and humanity, hardness and pride; in place of happiness, the heroic life; in place of decadence, creation. This indeed, as Nietzsche insisted, is no philosophy for the masses, or rather, it assigns the masses to their proper place as beings of a lower order whose healthy instinct is to

follow their leader. Once this healthy instinct is corrupted the masses create only a slave morality, a fiction of humanity, pity, and self-abnegation, which in part reflects their own inferiority but is more truly a subtle poison, an invention of servile cunning, to sterilize the powers of the creators. For there is nothing that the common man fears or hates so much as the disruptive force of originality.[57]

Conclusions

Far from merely being selfish individualists we have clearly evolved a distinctive human nature for co-operation and sympathy in social life, and we find everywhere some norms for regulating competition and personal conduct which are necessary for any viable society. But morality involves much more than basic co-operation and prohibitions on theft, violence, and cheating within the group. As societies become more complex, they offer all sorts of opportunities for conquest and the enjoyment of power and status, wealth, luxury, and every kind of physical indulgence, oppressing and exploiting the weak, and for hatred and cruelty, all of which are also very appealing to human nature. Human nature, therefore, is not enough to guide many of our moral choices, and we may actually have to struggle against our natural impulses and the pressures of society in order to do the right thing. Trying to discover in general terms what 'the right thing' is, however, raises many profound questions about the meaning of life, Man's place in the universe, and how we can attain happiness. It is here that religion has a distinctive contribution to make.

Rather than the traditional religious image of morality as simply the commandments of a deity, it is far more fruitful to ask how adding the spiritual dimension of existence to the material dimension changes the sort of ethical system we can have. It indicates, first of all, that Man exists in a universe of meaning and purpose, and where goodness has an objective value; that the individual members of each society have souls as well as material bodies; and that a Supreme Being whom we call God also has a personal relation to each human being. In turn, this brings them all into a new universal relationship with one another through the agency of God, into a kind of 'second commonwealth', regardless of the societies of which they are legal members. They each, through their association with God, have a special dignity which is distinct from their social status, and an individual purpose in living that is related to God as well as to their society. As God loves each individual, individuals attain happiness by loving God and their neighbour. But developing personal virtue is an integral part of loving God and one's neighbour, and two of the main conditions of happiness are that the material is subordinated to the spiritual and the worship of self is replaced by humility. Religious ethics therefore emphasise virtue rather than secular principles such as rights, justice, and utility. Individual virtue benefits society, but society must also respect the dignity of its individual members, and religion has a special value in standing above all societies and so in balancing the claims of society and the individual. The values that are important for society, like power, wealth, and success, are also very different from those that are important to God, which is why religion can provide a distinctive critique of society and its values.

None of this means, of course, that religion must therefore be true. But if it isn't, and if materialism is taken to its logical conclusion, then we must accept that Man is no different from other animals in a basically Darwinian world, and also that the mind, free will, consciousness, personal identity, and purpose are all illusions, so that we cease to be human at all, and the very meaning of ethics disappears. Social life is based on the assumptions of consciousness, personal identity, and free will, and without them simply becomes unintelligible. It is therefore very striking that so many atheists, and especially those who call themselves Humanists, are apparently unwilling to accept this logical conclusion of materialism, though it is not clear on what grounds, and have been outspoken defenders of their own ethical views, regardless of the implications of materialism. These are that reason and science, alone and unconstrained by a religious world-view, are deeply anti-human.

We are now in the position to take up the claim that one does not need God to be good, and the challenge of the atheist journalist Christopher Hitchens: 'Name one moral action performed by a believer that could not have been done by a non-believer.' To complete this, however, we first need to add a further challenge: 'Name one immoral action performed by a nonbeliever that *could* have been done by a believer'. But before we continue we also need to remove an ambiguity here. Hitchens seems to assume that a 'moral' action is one that both believers and unbelievers would regard as good, those 'common decencies' such as paying one's debts, telling the truth, or keeping one's promises. There are indeed many such forms of behaviour that people of all religions and none would commend as necessary for the preservation of the social order. We can therefore agree with Hitchens that there is no reason to expect any special differences here between the conduct of believers and unbelievers, and the same would be true as well of many immoral actions that are also generally agreed to threaten the social order, such as theft, rape, and murder. To this extent it is clear that one does not need God to be good, and we also have to consider the influence of the traditional culture. So it is not particularly surprising that countries such as Scandinavia where religious believers are relatively few, but are still influenced by their Protestant cultural heritage, may nevertheless have low levels of crime.

The real differences, however, would arise over what believers and unbelievers would regard as moral and immoral in the first place. (In what follows, I will take 'believer' to mean 'Christian', since I am not qualified to speak for other religions.) An atheist might very well be an Objectivist, for example, and would not consider risking his own life, or even serious discomfort, to save that of a stranger, and would be equally unwilling to perform unpaid public service, or go and help the poor in a Third World country, or in fact do anything that did not have a selfish motive. Forgiving one's enemies would be eccentric, and loving them unthinkable, while taking revenge on them would be very appealing. The distinction between spiritual and material values would be meaningless, and pride, selfishness, and general narcissism would seem perfectly natural, so that being a winner, social success, wealth, luxury and power would all be eminently desirable and worth struggling for at any cost, because life has no other meaning, whereas humility and self-denial would be morbid and ridiculous. In the same way it would be far more sensible to go with the crowd than to make oneself unpopular by standing up for some moral principle. Human life as such would have no special value, universal rights are a fantasy, and not only abortion and infanticide but the extermination of the old, sick, mentally retarded and no doubt other 'burdens on society' would be perfectly justifiable as well. The atheist need have no particular concern with the poor, and could easily join Professor Nietzsche in regarding them as contemptible losers and natural inferiors, who are there to be exploited as a matter of course. Totalitarian states, particularly those driven by the belief in Reason and Planning, would also be quite acceptable, especially if the atheist could be employed as one of the planners or enforcers, and the use of terror and the extermination of the enemies of the state would be a rational policy, whereas being a martyr for one's beliefs or a conscientious objector would be absurd. Since there is no such thing as human dignity, techniques of mind control and physical torture for the purposes of the state would be quite acceptable. Warfare, especially between different ethnic groups, is perfectly natural, and the conquest or extermination of foreigners, especially to seize their natural resources like oil, would be a normal strategy of international relations.

We must be clear that 'could' and 'could not' here refer to *principles*, not to the actual behaviour of individuals. Of course, the atheist does not *have* to behave in any of these ways but there is nothing in atheism itself which prohibits them either. It would be perfectly *possible* for an atheist to jump into a river to save a stranger from drowning, but this could not be justified by his atheist principles but simply explained by the sort of person he was. On the other hand, plenty of Christians have committed appalling acts – perhaps we can think here of paedophile priests – but there is no way in which these could be justified by an appeal to Christian principles. Indeed, they might invite Jesus' rebuke 'Depart from me, you accursed, I never knew you.' Christian principles also forbid participation in any of the objectivist or totalitarian philosophies discussed in the previous chapter, even though many Christian individuals have in fact been seduced into doing this either through weakness of character or confusion of mind. So we seem to have accumulated a rather large checklist both of good actions that atheists would see no reason to do, and of things that atheists could do without compunction that ought to repel the believer.

We need to remember, however, that most people, even if they are unbelievers, are most unlikely, unless they are intellectual fanatics, to base their lives on the theoretical principles of atheism alone. Conduct is influenced by many other factors besides beliefs, not only by culture and upbringing but by basic personality. There is no psychological law that I am aware of that says someone who is temperamentally kind must necessarily be either religious or non-religious, and I have a number of very decent atheist friends. Indeed, I was an atheist myself for many years in my youth and so am well aware of the absurdity of demonising every unbeliever.

Notes

Notes for Introduction

1. An atheist advertising campaign in 2009. The word 'probably' was inserted to avoid breaching the Advertising Code.

2. Humanists revere natural science for its intellectual humility, its willingness to follow the evidence and its readiness to discard cherished beliefs when they are contradicted by the facts. Dawkins, for example, describes how his memory of a senior biologist admitting in public that he had been wrong for years about a feature of cell structure 'still brings a lump to my throat' (Dawkins 2006:284). One would broadly accept the humanist picture of the natural sciences but not, however, when evolutionary biologists discuss the inherently controversial subject of Man. In my experience of dealing with them for more than thirty years they have a clear ideological agenda, and sometimes seem as impervious to argument as religious fundamentalists. Here I thoroughly agree with my fellow anthropologist, Professor Tim Ingold: 'I have found neo-Darwinian selectionists peculiarly intolerant of any intellectual challenge to their point of view. They simply assume it to be unassailable and refuse to discuss it further. Their favourite ploy, of course, is to brand anyone who doesn't fall into line as a crypto-Creationist' (Ingold 2000:2). Not much occasion for 'lumps in the throat' here, then.

Notes for Chapter 1

1. Pagel, M., & Bodmer, W. 2003. 'A naked ape would have fewer parasites'. *Proceedings of the Royal Society of London*, B, (Suppl) 270, 117-119.

2. Pagel & Bodmer 2003:118.

3. I am not referring, of course, to the use of sewn skin

clothing from about 30,000 years ago worn by our predecessors in the Arctic.

4. Curtis 2013.

5. See Cohen 1989:98-9

6. Carrier & Morgan 2014.

7. e.g. Orians 1980, Orians & Heerwagen 1992.

8. Bronowski 2012:3-4.

9. Wallace 1871:356.

10. Everett 2008.

11. Denny 1986:133

12. Devlin 2000:3.

13. Geertz 1973:49.

14. Dawkins 1978:2-3.

15. Alexander 1987:3.

16. Sober & Wilson 1998:27. They provide a detailed explanation of how altruism can in fact evolve through group selection (pp. 64-79), and show that Hamilton subsequently changed his mind on the subject, particularly through the work of George Price, whose equation demonstrated how group selection could work.

17. Mencius, the major Confucian teacher, held that people are naturally compassionate: 'Suppose a man were, all of a sudden, to see a child on the verge of falling into a well. He would certainly be moved to compassion, not because he wanted to get in the good graces of the parents, nor because he wished to win the praises of his fellow villagers or friends, nor yet because he disliked the cry of the child' (*Mencius* 2.A.6). Because the man has 'all of a sudden' to make a decision he has no time to be influenced by selfishness or extraneous factors, and Mencius believes, I think rightly, that the normal person will act with spontaneous compassion to save the child.

18. '...it is in this domain [of sympathy] that striking continuities exist between humans and other animals. To be vicari-

ously affected by the emotions of others must be very basic, because these reactions have been reported for a great variety of animals and are often immediate and uncontrollable. They probably first emerged with parental care, in which vulnerable individuals are fed and protected. In many animals they stretch beyond this domain, however, to relations among unrelated adults.' (de Waal 2009:14-15).

19. Wilson 1993: 46, and Sober & Wilson 1998:262, Stotland 1969, Krebs 1975.
20. Eisenberg & Mussen 1989:46.
21. Tiger & Fox 1971:32-3.
22. Boehm 1999:30.
23. ibid., 5.
24. Wilson 2004:91.
25. Boehm 1999:88.
26. Skinner 1974:10.
27. Skinner 1971:15.
28. Tooby & Cosmides 1992:20.
29. Crick 1994:3.
30. Tooby & Cosmides 1992:20-21.
31. For a detailed discussion of 'emergence' as Dawkins uses it, see Strawson 2006:12-21.
32. Polkinghorne 2011: 3-4.
33. Blackmore 2005:81.
34. McCoy 2004:41, citing Finnis 1983.
35. Russell 1948a:240.
36. e.g. Baker & Goetz 2011.
37. Polkinghorne 2011: 71-2.
38. Polkinghorne 2011: 72.
39. Penrose 1999:123-25.
40. Wilson 2004:78
41. Dawkins 1978:205, and see also Lumsden & Wilson 1981; Richerson & Boyd 1985, 2006.
42. 'Both biological and cultural evolution involve *nothing but*

[my emphasis] the differential propagation of instructions: soma [organism] and society are merely an instruction's way to make more instructions. They [soma and society] are epiphenomena. Evolution is not about the survival of the individual carrier of an instruction; it is about instructions competing with each other to increase their (respective) frequencies.' (Barkow 1978:11).

43. 'To start to think memetically we have to make a giant flip in our minds just as biologists had to do when taking on the idea of the selfish gene. Instead of thinking of our ideas as our own creations, and as working for us, we have to think of them as autonomous selfish memes, working only to get themselves copied. We humans, because of our powers of imitation, have become just the physical 'hosts' needed for memes to get around. This is how the world looks from a "meme's eye view".' (Blackmore 1999:8).

44. Jacob 1982:23).

45. See also Rees 2000, Davies 2007, Kauffman 1995)

46. Medawar 1984:66.

47. Dawkins 2006:50.

48. Dawkins 2006:36.

Notes for Chapter 2

1. I do not however accept the claim by Hauser (2008) that we have an innate moral faculty, a 'universal moral grammar', basically similar to Chomsky's generative grammar for language. Just as our innate generative grammar allows us to construct a limitless variety of correct sentences, so Hauser proposes that our universal moral grammar has 'a capacity that enables each individual to unconsciously and automatically evaluate a limitless variety of actions in terms of principles that dictate what is permissible, obligatory, or forbidden' (41). Moral systems evolve in relation to social complexity (Hallpike 2004), and are inextricably involved

with the whole of social relations, whereas the grammatical rules of a language are completely isolated and have no connection at all with the rest of the culture. They do not evolve in relation to social complexity, except in the size of their vocabulary. '[N]o sign of evolution from a simpler to a more complex state of development can be found in any of the thousands of languages known to exist or to have existed in the past' (Lyons 1977 (I):85). Again, individuals' understanding of moral issues undergoes cognitive development until the late teens or twenties, in the right social milieu, whereas a complete mastery of grammar is typically attained by children of around five or six. Languages and moral systems therefore appear to be completely different things.

2. de Waal 2009: 18.

3. Well illustrated, for example, in the following statement by Professor Sir Edmund Leach:
    'The content of moral prohibitions varies wildly not only as between one society and another but even within the same society as between one social class and another or between one historical period and another. Breathing apart, it is difficult to think of any kind of human activity which has not, at one time or another, been considered wrong' (Leach 1968:49).

4. Macaulay 1952 [1839]:614.

5. Dawkins 1978:212. Dawkins seems to have got the idea that faith involves believing things 'in the teeth of the evidence' from a statement by Tertullian (see *A Devil's Chaplain*, p.139), one of the early Church Fathers, 'It is certain because it is impossible'. But as Alister McGrath (2005:99-101) points out, Dawkins entirely misunderstands the point that Tertullian was making. He was referring to the Resurrection and giving rhetorical exaggeration to an argument of Aristotle 'that an extraordinary claim may well be true,

precisely because it is so out of the ordinary' (ibid., 101). Rather in the same way, we may say of some extraordinary event, 'You couldn't make it up'.

6. Grayling 2013:18-19.
7. Park 2008:215.
8. Huxley 1950:269.
9. Ward 2004:157.
10. Tylor 1871(I):383.
11. Ward 2004:105
12. Dawkins 2006:16.
13. Bellah 1970:21.
14. Ward 2004: 21
15. Bellah 1970:23.
16. James 1962: 56.
17. Berndt & Berndt 1964: 188.
18. Ward 2004: 47.
19. Trigger 2003:671.
20. On this see for example Armstrong 1999:69-84
21. Bellah 1970:35.
22. Hallpike 2004:303-5; Snell 1960.
23. Momigliano 1975:8-9.
24. Huxley 1950:1.
25. Taken from Encyclopaedia Britannica, 'Logos'. See also Marsh 1968:96-7, Newbigin 1982:3.
26. Heater 2004:12.
27. Bellah 1970: 22.
28. ibid., 33.
29. James 1962:353.
30. I quote a number of very well-known sayings of Jesus without further reference, and in the knowledge that Biblical scholars have expressed doubts about the accuracy with which some of them report the actual words that Jesus would have used.
31. James 1962:170-1.

32. ibid., 367.
33. ibid., 401.
34. Sabatier, quoted by James 1952: 443-4.
35. Misra 1984: 92.
36. Munro 1985:3.
37. *The Week*, 2014, Issue 964, p.57.
38. Misra 1984: 25.
39. Ward 2004: 91.
40. Diogenes Laertius vii. 88, Long 1986: 179.
41. Fakhry 1991:111.
42. James 1962:268-9.
43. Bodde 1991: 315.
44. Dial.3: 185. Misra 1984: 80.
45. *Manu* 2.162.
46. Izutsu 1966:17-8.
47. James 1952: 443.
48. Long 1986:70, 147.
49. Dasgupta 1940:550.
50. McCoy 2001:144.
51. J.H.Newman, *Meditations and Devotions*, 400-1, cited in R.Murray, *The Good Pagan's Failure* (1962:150).
52. cited in Huxley 1950: 119.
53. cited in Huxley 1950:208.
54. cited in Huxley 1950:279.

Notes for Chapter 3

1. Eamon 1994:60.
2. White 1978:27.
3. 'The most pervasive route through which these ideas passed into Latin medieval thought was Augustine [AD 354-430], for whom the *naturales leges* which God had ordained were the laws of measures, numbers and weights. He applied the concept of natural laws, or laws of nature, to the motions of the heavenly bodies, the generation of living

things, and the development of the world itself pregnant with things to come. God could then be discovered in the great open book of nature, as well as in the revealed book of Holy Scripture. These ideas were to become fundamental principles of Western medieval and early modern natural philosophy' (Crombie 1996:470).

4. Needham 1956:582.

5. An excellent discussion of the relations between science and religion can be found in McGrath 2005:139-59.

6. Crick 2004:95.

7. Porter 2001:12.

8. Porter 2001:33.

9. G.M.Young, 'Introduction' to *Selected Poems of Thomas Hardy*, 1953, p. xviii.

10. Branden 1984:12.

11. Smelser 1989:1.

12. Baumeister et al. 2003:4.

13. ibid., 2.

14. ibid., 2003:8.

15. ibid., 2003:1.

16. Boden et al., 337.

17. Baumeister et al. 2003:6.

18. Wilson 1993:250.

19. Jacob 1982:68.

20. 'Mill described Bentham's striking lack of understanding of other people. He wrote of: "the incompleteness of his [Bentham's] own mind as a representative of universal human nature. In many of the most natural and strongest feelings of human nature he had no sympathy; from many of its graver experiences he was altogether cut off; and the faculty by which one mind understands a mind different from itself, and throws itself into the feelings of that other mind, was denied him by his deficiency of Imagination."' (Lucas & Sheehan 2006:6-7).

21. George et al. 2000:111.
22. See Koenig & Cohen 2002 for a detailed support for these claims.
23. Smiles 1877:iii-iv.
24. Bradley 2007:14.
25. See Scotland 1997.
26. Dawkins 2006:306.
27. Ward 2004:182.
28. Dumont 1970:263, *n*.1a.
29. Tawney 1938:207.
30. 'The state of nature has a law of nature to govern it, which obliges everyone: and reason, which is that law, teaches all mankind, who will but consult it, that all being equal and independent, no one ought to harm another in his life, health, liberty, or possessions. For men being all the workmanship of one Omnipotent, and infinitely wise Maker; all the servants of one Sovereign Master, sent into the world by His order and about His business, they are His property, whose workmanship they are...' (Locke *Second Treatise of Government*, 1988:271).
31. Russell 1948b: 649.
32. Paine [1792]1995:117, 118.
33. Dumont 1970:5.
34. Kohlberg 1984:177, 179.
35. Nozick 1974:ix.
36. Bawer 2012:84-8.
37. ibid., 314.
38. 'The Fat Acceptance movement', Wikipedia.
39. From review of 'Far From the Tree' by Andrew Solomon, by Sam Leith, *Spectator* 16. February 2013, p.34.
40. Giubilini et al., 2013:262-3.
41. ibid., 263.
42. Gregg 2013.
43. Haidt 2012:96.

44. ibid., 97.
45. ibid., 99-100.
46. ibid., 100.

Notes for Chapter 4

1. Dawkins 2006:273.
2. See Weikart 1995 on a letter from Darwin supporting economic individualism.
3. Rand 1982:12.
4. In Rand 1964: 42-3.
5. ibid., 43-4
6. Baumeister et al. 2003:6.
7. Raskin & Hall 1979:590. See also Watson et al. 1984.
8. Piff 2014:35.
9. Piff et al. 201 2:4086.
10. Skinner 1971:15. At this point it is important to note that even if one accepted Skinner's belief that non-material mental processes are inherently impossible, that in itself seems no justification for dismissing the possibility of mediating states of the *brain* that are neurological in nature. Skinner, however, is not troubled by this objection; he does refer very briefly to the brain, but concludes that 'What [the physiologist] discovers cannot invalidate the laws of a science of behavior, but it will make the picture of human action more nearly complete' (Skinner 1974:215).
11. Skinner 1962:221.
12. Skinner 1971:21.
13. ibid, 200-201).
14. His most effective point was the 'poverty of the stimulus' argument: young children clearly have an inherent mastery of grammatical principles that enables them to construct sentences that are quite different from anything they have heard before, and so cannot be the result of any previous reinforcement (Chomsky 1959:42-44).

15. Chomsky 1959: 31.
16. quoted in Chomsky 1959:38.
17. Skinner 1974:149.
18. Miller 2003.
19. Engels [2010]:53.
20. K.Marx & F.Engels. *Manifesto of the Communist Party.* 1969:72. Moscow: Progress Publishers.
21. Berlin 1980:170. I am most obliged to Dr Henry Hardy for locating this quotation for me.
22. Kuusinen 1961: 832-3.
23. ibid., 868.
24. Bales 1969.
25. Dikötter 2010:298, 334.
26. *Free at Last*, p.371.
27. 'Michael Ignatieff interviews Eric Hobsbawm'. BBC. 24 October 1994 The Late Show.
28. Goldberg 2007: 159.
29. Waite 1993: 87.
30. ibid., 75.
31. ibid., 80.
32. ibid., 83.
33. Waite 1993:3.
34. cited in Haffner 2003:79.
35. Haffner 2003:126.
36. Waite 1993: 20.
37. quoted in Haffner 2003:160.
38. Waite 1993: 34.
39. Darwin 2011 [1871]:84-5.
40. ibid., 87.
41. Crook points out that before and after World War I, there was also an opposite school of thought that used Darwinian arguments in favour of peace, 'A sub-genre of "anti-war evolution" employed specifically evolutionary, and especially Darwinian, discourse to counter the war school's

use of struggle-based analogies from nature. Peace biology expounded an optimistic world-view based upon Darwin's holistic ecology, and used new disciplines such as eugenics to demonstrate that war was a biological disaster for mankind' (Crook 1994:2). It had very little influence, however.

42. quoted in Weikart 1993:473.

43. Weikart 1993:482.

44. Weikart 1993: 485.

45. Manheim 1969: viii.

46. quoted in James 1962: 360-1.

47. Hollingdale 2002:75.

48. *The Gay Science*, 4, quoted in Hollingdale, 141.

49. Hollingdale 2002:57.

50. ibid., 162-3

51. ibid., 187.

52. *Beyond Good and Evil*, quoted in Hollingdale 2002:187.

53. quoted in Waite 1993:276.

54. *Genealogy of Morals* I, 11, quoted in Hollingdale 2002:189.

55. *Genealogy of Morals* II, 17, quoted in Hollingdale 2002:189.

56. *Beyond Good and Evil*, 258, quoted in Hollingdale 2002:191.

57. Sabine 1960:720-21.

References

Alexander, R.D. 1987. *The Biology of Moral Systems*. New York: Aldine de Gruyter.

Armstrong, K. 1999. *A History of God*. London. London: Vintage Books.

Baker, M.C. & Goetz, S. (Eds.) 2011. *The Soul Hypothesis. Investigations into the existence of the soul*. New York: Continuum.

Bales, J.D. 1969. *Communism and the Reality of Moral Law*. NJ: Craig Press.

Barkow, J.H. 1978. 'Culture and sociobiology', *American Anthropologist*, 80, 5-20.

Baumeister, R.F., & Vohs, K.D. 2001. 'Narcissism as addiction to esteem', *Psychological Inquiry*, 12(4), 206-10.

Baumeister, R.F., et al. 2003. 'Does high self-esteem cause better performance, inter-personal success, happiness, or healthier lifestyles?', *Psychological Science in the Public Interest*, 4(1), 1-44.

Bawer, B. 2012. *The Victims' Revolution*. New York: Harper Collins.

Bellah, R.N. 1970. 'Religious evolution', in *Beyond Belief. Essays on religion in a post-traditional world*. 20-52. New York: Harper & Row.

Berlin, I. 1980. *Personal Impressions*. London: Hogarth Press.

Berndt, R.M., & C.H. 1964. *The World of the First Australians*. London: Angus & Robertson.

Blackmore, S. 1999. *The Meme Machine*. Oxford University Press.

Blackmore, S. 2005. *Consciousness: an Introduction*. London, Routledge.

Bodde, D. 1991. *Chinese Thought, Society, and Science*. University of Hawaii Press.

Boehm, C. 1999. *Hierarchy in the Forest: the evolution of egalitarian behavior*. Harvard University Press.

Boden, J.M. et al., 2008. 'Does adolescent self-esteem predict later life outcomes? A test of the causal role of self-esteem', *Development and Psychopathology*, 20, 319-39.

Bradley, I. 2007. *Enlightened Entrepreneurs. Business ethics in Victorian Britain*. (2nd Ed.) Oxford: Lion Books.

Branden, N. 1969 *The Psychology of Self-Esteem*. Nash Publishing.

Bronowski, J. 2012. *The Ascent of Man*. London: Folio Society.

Bullock, A. 1962. *Hitler: A Study in Tyranny*. London: Pelican.

Carrier, D., & Morgan, M.H. 2014. 'Protective buttressing of the hominin face',*Biological Reviews*, June (online Early View).

Chomsky, N. 1959. Review of B.F.Skinner 'Verbal Behavior', *Language*, 35, 26-58.

Cohen, M.N. 1989. *Health and the Rise of Civilization*. Yale University Press.

Crick, F. 1994. *The Astonishing Hypothesis. The scientific search for the soul*. NewYork: Touchstone.

Crick, F. 2004. *Of Molecules and Men*. New York: Prometheus Books.

Crombie, A.C. 1996. *Science, Art and Nature in Medieval and Modern Thought*. London: Hambledon Press.

Crook, P. 1994. *Darwinism, War, and History: The debate over the biology of war and the "Origin of Species" to the First World War*. New York: Cambridge University Press.

Curtis, V. 2013. 'Why manners matter', *New Scientist*, 2935, 28-9.

Darwin, C. 1902. [1859] *The Origin of Species by means of natural selection*.6th Ed. London: Murray.

Darwin, C. 2011.[1871]. *The Descent of Man*. Pacific Publishing Studio.

Dasgupta, S. 1940. *History of Indian Philosophy*. I. Cambridge University Press.

Davies, P. 2007. *The Goldilocks Enigma. Why is the universe just right for life?* London: Penguin.

Dawkins, R. 1978. *The Selfish Gene*. London: Paladin Books.

Dawkins, R. 2006. *The God Delusion*. London: Bantam Press.

Day, V. 2008. *The Irrational Atheist*. Dallas: Benbella Books Inc.

Dennett, D. 1991. *Consciousness Explained*. Boston: Little, Brown.

Dennett, D.1995. *Darwin's Dangerous Idea. Evolution and the meanings of life*. London: Penguin Books.

Denny, J.P.1986. 'Cultural ecology of mathematics: Ojibway and Inuit hunters', in *Native American Mathematics*, Ed. M.P.Closs. 129-80. University of Texas Press.

Dervic, K. et al. 2004. 'Religious affiliation and suicide attempts', *American Journal of Psychiatry*, 161, 2303-2308.

Devlin, K. 2000. *The Math Gene*. London: Weidenfeld & Nicolson.

Dumont, L. 1970. *Homo Hierarchicus: The caste system and its implications*.Tr. M. Sainsbury. London: Weidenfeld & Nicolson.

Durkheim, E. 1952. [1897] *Suicide. A study in sociology*. London: Routledge & Kegan Paul.

Eamon, W. 1994. *Science and the Secrets of Nature*. Princeton University Press.

Eisenberg, N., & Mussen, P.A. 1989, *The Roots of Prosocial Behavior in Children*. Cambridge University Press.

Engels, F. 2010. [1902] *The Origin of the Family, Private Property and the State*. Memphis, Tennessee: General Books.

Everett, D. 2008. *Don't Sleep, There Are Snakes. Life and language in the Amazonian jungle*. London: Profile Books.

Fakhry, M. 1991. *Ethical Theories in Islam*. Leiden: Brill.

Fest, J. 1970. *The Face of the Third Reich. Portraits of the Nazi leadership*. Tr. M.Bullock. New York: Pantheon Books.

Finnis, J.1983. *Fundamentals of Ethics*. Oxford: Clarendon Press.

Geertz, C. 1973. *The Interpretation of Cultures*. New York: Basic Books.

George, L.K., et al. 2000. 'Spirituality and health: what we know, what we need to know', *Journal of Social and Clinical Psychology*, 19(1), 102-16.

Goldberg, J. 2007. *Liberal Fascism*. London: Penguin Books.

Grayling, A.C. 2013. *The God Argument: the Case against Religion and for Humanism*. London: Bloomsbury.

Gregg, J. 2013. *Are Dolphins Really Smart? The mammal behind the myth*. Oxford University Press.

Giubilini, A. & Minerva, F. 2013. 'After-birth abortion: why should the baby live?', *Journal of Medical Ethics*, 39, 261-3.

Haffner, S. 2003. *The Meaning of Hitler*. London: Phoenix.

Haidt, J. 2012. *The Righteous Mind. Why good people are divided by politics and religion*. London: Allen Lane.

Hallpike, C.R. 1977. *Bloodshed and Vengeance in the Papuan Mountains*. Oxford: Clarendon Press.

Hallpike, C.R. 1979. *The Foundations of Primitive Thought*. Oxford: Clarendon Press.

Hallpike, C.R. 1984 'The relevance of the theory of inclusive fitness to human society', *Journal of Social and Biological Structures*, 7, 131-44.

Hallpike, C.R. 1986. *The Principles of Social Evolution*. Oxford: Clarendon Press.

Hallpike, C.R. 2004. *The Evolution of Moral Understanding*. Alton, Hants:Prometheus Research Group.

Hallpike, C.R. 2008a. *The Konso of Ethiopia. A study of the values of an East Cushitic people*. (2nd Ed.) Bloomington, Indiana: AuthorHouse.

Hallpike, C.R. 2008b. *How We Got Here*. Bloomington, Indiana: AuthorHouse.

Hallpike, C.R. 2011a. 'Memetics: a Darwinian pseudo-science', *On Primitive Society, and other forbidden topics*, 104-27. Bloomington, Indiana: AuthorHouse.

Hallpike,C.R. 2011b. 'The weakness of adaptive explanations', *On Primitive Society, and other forbidden topics*, 128-52. Bloomington, Indiana: AuthorHouse.

Hallpike, C.R.2011c. 'Some anthropological objections to evolutionary psychology', *On Primitive Society, and other forbidden topics*, 214-55. Bloomington, Indiana: AuthorHouse.

Hauser, M.D. 2006. *Moral Minds: How nature designed our universal sense of right and wrong*. New York: Harper Collins.

Heater, D. 2004. *Citizenship. The civic ideal in world history, politics and education.* 3rd Ed. Manchester University Press.

Hitler, A. 1969. *Mein Kampf.* Tr. R.Manheim. London: Hutchinson.

Hollingdale, R.J. 2002. *Nietzsche: the Man and His Philosophy.* (2nd Ed.) Cambridge University Press.

Huxley, A. 1950. *The Perennial Philosophy.* London: Chatto & Windus.

Huxley, T.H. 1894. *Evolution and Ethics, and other essays.* London: Macmillan.

Ingold, T. 2000. 'The poverty of selectionism', *Anthropology Today*, 16(3), 1-2.

Izutsu, T. 1966. *Ethico-Religious Concepts in the Qur'an.* McGill University Press.

Jacob, F. 1982. *The Possible and the Actual.* New York: Pantheon.

James, William. 1962. *The Varieties of Religious Experience.* London: Fontana.

Kauffman, S. 1995. *At Home in the Universe. The search for the laws of self-organization and complexity.* Oxford University Press.

Keynes, J.M. 1949. *Two Memoirs.* London: Hart-Davis.

Kohlberg, L. 1984. *The Psychology of Moral Development.* San Francisco: Harper & Row.

Koenig, H.G. & Cohen, H.J. 2002. *The Link between Religion and Health. Psychoneuroimmunology and the faith factor.* Oxford University Press.

Krebs, D.L. 1975. 'Empathy and altruism', *Journal of Personality and Social Psychology*, 32, 1134-1136.

Kurtz, P. 2008. *Forbidden Fruit: the Ethics of Secularism.* New York: Prometheus Books.

Kuusinen, O. (Ed.) 1961. *Fundamentals of Marxism-Leninism.* London: Lawrence & Wishart.

Leach, E.R. 1968. *A Runaway World?* 1967 Reith Lectures. Oxford University Press.

Locke, J. 1988 [1689] *Two Treatises of Government.* Ed. P.Laslett.

Cambridge University Press.

Long, A.A. 1986. *Hellenistic Philosophy. Stoics, Epicureans, Sceptics.* 2nd Ed. London: Duckworth.

Lucas, P., & Sheehan, A. 2006. 'Asperger's syndrome, and the eccentricity and genius of Jeremy Bentham', *Journal of Bentham Studies*, 8, 1-37.

Lumsden, C.J., & Wilson, E.O. 1981. *Genes, Mind, and Culture.* Harvard University Press.

Lyons, J. 1977. *Semantics.* (2 vols.). Cambridge University Press.

Macaulay, T.B. 1952 [1839]. 'Gladstone on Church and State', in *Macaulay, Prose and Poetry.* Ed. G.M.Young. 609-60. London: Rupert Hart-Davis.

Manheim, R. 1969. *Translator's Note* to Mein Kampf. vii-x. London: Hutchinson. Markham, F.M.H. 1952. *Henri Comte de Saint-Simon. Selected Writings.* Oxford: Blackwell.

Marsh, J. 1968. *The Gospel of Saint John.* London: Penguin.

McCoy, A. 2004. *An Intelligent Person's Guide to Christian Ethics.* London: Continuum.

McGrath, A. 2005. *Dawkins' God. Genes, memes, and the meaning of life.* Oxford:Blackwell.

Medawar, P. 1984. *Pluto's Republic.* Oxford University Press.

Mill, J.S. 1885. *Three Essays on Religion.* 3rd Ed. London: Longmans, Green, & Co.

Miller, G.A. 2003. 'The cognitive revolution: a historical perspective', *Trends in Cognitive Sciences*, 7 (3), 141-44).

Misra, G.S.P.1984. *The Development of Buddhist Ethics.* Delhi: Munshiram Mandharlal Publishers.

Momigliano, A. 1975. *Alien Wisdom. The limits of Hellenization.* Cambridge University Press.

Morgan, L.H. 1978. [1877]. *Ancient Society.* Palo Alto: New York Labor News.

Munro, D.S. 1985. 'Introduction', to *Individualism and Holism. Studies in Confucian and Taoist values.* Ed. D.S.Munro, 1-32. University of Michigan Press.

Murray, R. 1962. *The Good Pagan's Failure*. London: Fontana.

Needham, J. 1956. *Science and Civilisation in China. vol. 2. History of Scientific Thought*. Cambridge University Press.

Newbigin, L. 1982. *The Light Has Come. An exposition of the Fourth Gospel*.Grand Rapids Michigan: Eerdmans Publishing Co.

Nozick, R. 1974. *Anarchy, State, and Utopia*. New York: Basic Books.

Orians, G.H. 1980. 'Habitat selection:general theory and applications to human behavior', in (Ed.) J.S.Lockard, *The Evolution of Social Behavior*, 49-66. Chicago: Elsevier.

Orians, G.H. and Heerwagen, J.H. 1992. 'Evolved responses to landscapes', in (Eds.) J.H.Barkow *et al. The Adapted Mind.*, 555-79. Oxford University Press.

Pagel, M., & Bodmer, W. 2003. 'A naked ape would have fewer parasites', *Proceedings of the Royal Society of London*, B, (Suppl) 270, 117-119.

Paine, J. 1995 [1791] *The Rights of Man*. Ed. Mark Philp. Oxford University Press.

Park, R. 2008. *Superstition: Belief in the Age of Science*. Princeton University Press.

Penrose, R. 1989. *The Emperor's New Mind*. Oxford University Press.

Piaget, J. 1965. *The Moral Judgment of the Child*. London: Routledge & Kegan Paul.

Piff, K. et al. 2012. 'Higher social class predicts increased unethical behavior', *Proceedings of National Academy of Sciences*, 109(11), 4086-4091.

Piff, K. 2014. 'Wealth and the inflated self: class, entitlement, and narcissism', *Personality and Psychology Bulletin*, 40(1), 34-43.

Polkinghorne, J. 2011. *Science and Religion in Quest of Truth*. London: SPCK

Porter, R. 2001. *The Enlightenment*. (2nd Ed.) New York: Palgrave.

Rand, A. 1964. *The Virtue of Selfishness. A new concept of egoism*. New York: Signet Books.

Rand, A. 1982. *Philosophy. Who Needs It?* New York: Bobbs-Merrill.

Raskin, R.N., & Hall, C.S. 1979. 'A narcissistic personality inventory', *Psychological Reports*, 45, 590.

Rawls, J.B. 1971. *A Theory of Justice.* Harvard University Press.

Rees, M. 2000. *Just Six Numbers. Deep forces that shape the universe.* London:Orion Books.

Richerson, P.J., & Boyd, R. 1985. *Culture and the Evolutionary Process.* University of Chicago Press.

Richerson, P.J., & Boyd, R. 2006. *Not By Genes Alone. How culture transformed human evolution.* University of Chicago Press.

Russell, B. 1948a. *Human Knowledge: Its Scope and Limits.* London: Routledge.

Russell, B. 1948b. *A History of Western Philosophy.* London: Allen & Unwin.

Sabine, G.H. 1960 *A History of Political Theory.* 3rd Ed. London: Harrap.

Scotland, N. 1997. 'Methodism and the English labour movement 1800-1906', *Anvil*,14(1), 36-48.

Sherif, M., and Sherif, C.W. 1953. 'Groups in harmony and tension', in *The Dynamics of Aggression*, (Eds.) E.Megargee and J.Hokanson, 190-210. Longman.

Simpson, G.G. 1966. 'The biological nature of man', *Science* (n.s.) 152:472-8.

Singer, P. 1989. 'All animals are equal', in *Animal Rights and Human Obligations* Eds. T.Regan & P.Singer, 148-62. New Jersey.

Singer, P. 2009. 'Morality, reason, and the rights of animals', in *Primates and Philosophers: How morality evolved.* Eds. F.de Waal, S.Macedo & J.Ober, 140-60. Princeton University Press.

Skinner, B.F. 1957. *Verbal Behavior.* Cambridge, MA: Prentice Hall.

Skinner, B.F. 1962. *Walden Two.* New York: Macmillan.

Skinner, B.F. 1971. *Beyond Freedom and Dignity.* Indianapolis: Hackett.

Skinner, B.F. 1974. *About Behaviorism.* London: Jonathan Cape.

Smelser, N.J.1989. 'Self-esteem and social problems: an intro-duction', in A.M.Mecca et al. (Eds) *The Social Importance of Self-Esteem*, 1-23. University of California Press.

Smiles, S. 1877. *Self-Help*. London: Murray.

Snell, B. 1960. *The Discovery of the Mind. The Greek origins of European thought*. Tr. T.G.Rosenmeyer. New York: Harper & Row.

Sober, E., & Wilson, D.S. 1998. *Unto Others: the evolution and psychology of unselfish behavior*. Harvard University Press.

Spencer, H. 1897. *The Principles of Ethics*. (vol.1) London: Williams & Norgate.

Stotland, E. 1969. 'Exploratory investigations of empathy', in L.Berkowitz (Ed.) *Advances in Experimental Social Psychology*, 4, 271-314. New York:Academic Press.

Strawson, G.F. 2006. 'Realistic monism: why physicalism entails panpsychism', in *Consciousness and its Place in Nature*. Ed. A Freeman, 3-31. Exeter: Imprint Academic.

Tawney, R.H. 1938. *Religion and the Rise of Capitalism*. London: Pelican.

Tiger, L., & Fox, R. 1971. *The Imperial Animal*. Toronto: McClelland & Stewart.

Tomasello, M. 2009. *Why We Cooperate*. MIT Press.

Tooby, J., & Cosmides, L. 1992. 'The psychological foundations of culture', in *The Adapted Mind. Evolutionary psychology and the generation of culture'*, Eds. J.H.Barkow, L.Cosmides., & J.Tooby, 19-136. Oxford University Press.

Trevor-Roper, H.R. 1952. *The Last Days of Hitler*. 2nd Ed. London: Pan Books.

Trigger, B. 2003. *Understanding Ancient Civilizations*. Cambridge University Press.

Twenge, J.M. & Campbell, W.K. 2009.*The Narcissism Epidemic. Living in the age of entitlement*. New York: Free Press.

Tylor, E.1871. *Primitive Culture* (2 vols). London: Murray.

de Waal, F. 2009. 'Morally evolved: primate social instincts, human morality, and veneer theory', in *Primates and Philosophers. How morality evolved*. Eds. F. de Waal, S.Macedo & J.Ober. 3-58. Princeton University Press.

Waite, G.L. 1993. *The Psychopathic God: Adolf Hitler*. New York: Da Capo Press.

Wallace, A.R. 1871. 'The limits of natural selection as applied to Man', Chapter X in his *Contributions to the Theory of Natural Selection*, 2nd Ed. 332-71. London: Macmillan.

Ward, K. 2004 *The Case for Religion*. Oxford: Oneworld Publications.

Watson, P.J. et al. 1984. 'Religious orientation, humanistic values, and narcissism', *Review of Religious Research*, 25(3), 257-64.

Weikart, R. 1993. 'The origins of Social Darwinism in Germany, 1859-1895', *Journal of the History of Ideas*, 54(3), 469-88.

Weikart, R. 1995. 'A recently discovered Darwin letter on Social Darwinism', *Isis*, 86(4), 609-11.

White, L. 1978. *Medieval Religion and Technology*. University of California Press.

Wilson, E.O. 2004. *On Human Nature*. 2nd Ed. Harvard University Press.

Wilson, J.Q. 1993. *The Moral Sense*. New York: Free Press.

Wrangham, R. 2009. *Catching Fire. How cooking made us human*. London: Profile.

Young, G.M. 1953. 'Introduction' to *Selected Poems of Thomas Hardy*. ix-xxxiv. London: Macmillan.

Circle Books

Circle is a symbol of infinity and unity. It's part of a growing list of imprints, including o-books.net and zero-books.net.

Circle Books aims to publish books in Christian spirituality that are fresh, accessible, and stimulating.

Our books are available in all good English language bookstores worldwide. If you can't find the book on the shelves, then ask your bookstore to order it for you, quoting the ISBN and title. Or, you can order online—all major online retail sites carry our titles.

To see our list of titles, please view www.Circle-Books.com, growing by 80 titles per year.

Authors can learn more about our proposal process by going to our website and clicking on Your Company > Submissions.

We define Christian spirituality as the relationship between the self and its sense of the transcendent or sacred, which issues in literary and artistic expression, community, social activism, and practices. A wide range of disciplines within the field of religious studies can be called upon, including history, narrative studies, philosophy, theology, sociology, and psychology. Interfaith in approach, Circle Books fosters creative dialogue with non-Christian traditions.

And tune into MySpiritRadio.com for our book review radio show, hosted by June-Elleni Laine, where you can listen to authors discussing their books.

MySpiritRadio